BILLY GRAHAM
Evangelistic Association
Always Good News.

Dear Friend,

I am pleased to send you this copy of *Heavenly Rewards: Living with Eternity in Sight* by Dr. Mark Hitchcock, a well-known Bible teacher, pastor, and author who has written several books on Bible prophecy.

The Bible is clear that salvation is a free gift for all who trust Jesus Christ as their Lord and Savior. But there is a lot about the honors in Heaven we may not fully understand. Not only will the Lord review our life on judgment day, His Word declares, *"The judgments of the Lord are true and righteous altogether. ... And in keeping them there is great reward"* (Psalm 19:9, 11, NKJV). Dr. Hitchcock reminds us that rewards for a life lived for His glory are part of God's plan, and His Word offers great motivation for living faithfully for Him each day.

For more than 70 years, God has used the Billy Graham Evangelistic Association and friends like you to reach people all over the world with the Gospel. I'm so thankful for the ways He has worked—and what He will do in the years ahead.

If you represent one of the lives the Lord has touched, we would love to hear from you. Your story has the power to impact the lives of so many others. May God richly bless you.

Sincerely,

Franklin Graham
President & CEO

If you would like to know more about our ministry, please contact us:

IN THE U.S.:
Billy Graham Evangelistic Association
1 Billy Graham Parkway
Charlotte, NC 28201-0001
BillyGraham.org
info@bgea.org
Toll-free: 1-877-247-2426

IN CANADA:
Billy Graham Evangelistic
  Association of Canada
20 Hopewell Way NE
Calgary, AB T3J 5H5
BillyGraham.ca
Toll-free: 1-888-393-0003

HEAVENLY
REWARDS

MARK HITCHCOCK

HARVEST HOUSE PUBLISHERS
EUGENE, OREGON

HEAVENLY REWARDS

MARK HITCHCOCK

HARVEST HOUSE PUBLISHERS
EUGENE, OREGON

This *Billy Graham Library Selection* special edition is published with
permission from Harvest House Publishers.

Unless otherwise indicated, all Scripture quotations are taken from the New American Standard Bible®, © 1960, 1962, 1963, 1968, 1971, 1972, 1973, 1975, 1977, 1995 by The Lockman Foundation. Used by permission. (www.Lockman.org)

Verses marked NIV are taken from the Holy Bible, New International Version®, NIV®. Copyright © 1973, 1978, 1984, 2011 by Biblica, Inc.® Used by permission. All rights reserved worldwide.

Verses marked KJV are taken from the Kings James Version of the Bible.

Verses marked TLB are taken from The Living Bible, copyright © 1971. Used by permission of Tyndale House Publishers, Inc., Carol Stream, Illinois 60188. All rights reserved.

Verses marked PHILLIPS are taken from J.B. Phillips: The New Testament in Modern English, Revised Edition. ©J.B. Phillips 1958, 1960, 1972. Used by permission of Macmillian Publishing Company.

Cover design by Brian Bobel Design

Cover photo © tusumaru; tatianzaets / iStock

Published in association with William K. Jensen Literary Agency, 119 Bampton Court, Eugene, Oregon 97404.

Heavenly Rewards
Copyright© 2019 by Mark Hitchcock
Published by Harvest House Publishers
Eugene, Oregon 97408
www.harvesthousepublishers.com

ISBN 978-0-7369-7653-4 (pbk.)
ISBN 978-0-7369-7654-1 (eBook)
ISBN: 978-1-593-28707-8 (BGEA edition)

Library of Congress Cataloging-in-Publication Data

Names: Hitchcock, Mark, 1959-author.
Title: Heavenly rewards / Mark Hitchcock.
Description: Eugene: Harvest House Publishers, 2019. | Includes
   bibliographical references.
Identifiers: LCCN 2018054819 (print) LCCN 2019009334 (ebook) | ISBN
   9780736976541 (ebook) | ISBN 9780736976534 (pbk.)
Subjects: LCSH: Reward (Theology)
Classification: LCC BT940 (ebook) | LCC BT940 .H58 2019 (print) | DDC
   234--dc23
LC record available at https://lccn.loc.gov/2018054819

Printed in the United States of America

19 20 21 22 23 24 25 26 27 / BP-AR / 10 9 8 7 6 5 4 3 2 1

Contents

Foreword by Greg Laurie

Ever since my son Christopher went to heaven in 2008, I have been much more heavenly minded. His unexpected early arrival there sent me searching deeper into the mysteries and wonders of heaven and our future with Christ. As a teacher, preacher, and evangelist, I'm more committed than ever to helping point people to Jesus and eternity with Him in heaven.

When I had the opportunity to read Mark Hitchcock's new book *Heavenly Rewards*, I was excited to do so. Not only is Mark a friend and well-respected Bible teacher and writer, he has a particular gifting for addressing the topics of the end times and eternity. I had never come across a book dedicated solely to the subject of heavenly rewards, so I was eager to read it.

Mark has done a thorough, balanced, and biblically accurate job of tackling this overlooked and sometimes misunderstood subject. With his conversational style of writing, peppered with many helpful illustrations and insights, Mark has helped me to have a better understanding of what lies ahead for the believer in heaven. Reading this book will do the same for you.

The fact that God desires to bless us with rewards—beyond the overwhelming gifts of His grace, mercy, and salvation—boggles the mind. And yet, as Mark well describes, "receiving rewards will be a sign of God's pleasure and approval of our lives here on earth."[1] God's heavenly rewards are also a reminder to us as believers that while we'll never face God's judgment, we will give an accounting of our lives to the Lord in heaven. God will evaluate our earthly lives, opportunities, ministries, and motives—and then He will reward us. As my friend Warren Wiersbe put it, "For the Christian, heaven isn't simply a *destination*; it's a *motivation*."[2] It gives me great pleasure to recommend this book to you!

Greg Laurie, senior pastor, Harvest Christian Fellowship; evangelist, Harvest Crusades and Harvest America

What Lies Ahead?

Over the past couple decades, I've had the privilege of speaking at many churches and prophecy conferences in the United States and around the world. I've spoken on a variety of topics related to the book of Revelation, future events, and signs of the times that are setting the stage for the coming of Christ. I've discovered that people everywhere are very interested in what lies ahead for themselves and for this world. One set of related topics I've also addressed is heaven, hell, and the afterlife. These subjects have universal appeal.

Several few years ago, I began to teach on the judgment seat of Christ (also known as the bema judgment) and the rewards believers will receive in heaven.

I had studied these topics in-depth for many years and been personally challenged by what Scripture says, so I decided to prepare a message on the future evaluation of the lives of God's people and their heavenly rewards. These quickly became my favorite topics to address at churches and conferences because they are so practical, focused, and hope-filled.

The response to this message continues to be overwhelming. The feedback has been some of the most positive I've ever received. The topics have truly resonated with people. For quite some time I've wanted to put this message into a book to give it a wider reach and impact. The folks at Harvest House have graciously partnered with me to bring this dream to fruition. For that I am truly grateful.

The book you're holding is the core of the message I've delivered numerous times, along with a substantial amount of additional material having to do with the future and final rewards.

I hope you enjoy reading this book as much as I've enjoyed writing it. And may all of us apply its message to our lives, living each day in light of that moment when we will stand before our Lord.

Dr. Mark Hitchcock

CHAPTER ONE

One Shot

Only one life, 'twill soon be past,
Only what's done for Christ will last.[1]

C.T. Studd

At death we put the signature on our
life's portrait. The paint dries.
The portrait's done. Ready or not.[2]

Randy Alcorn

The famed Buffalo Bill Wild West Show performed throughout Europe during the final years of the nineteenth century and landed in Berlin, Germany, in 1899. The German people, like others in Europe, turned out by the thousands to see the Wild West Show. A smashing hit wherever it went, the show featured several entertainers with star power, but none was more compelling than Annie Oakley. Standing less than five feet tall, Oakley was known as "Little Sure Shot," a name she was given by Sitting Bull. She beat any male sharpshooter who dared to challenge her. Oakley had many amazing sharpshooting tricks as part of her act. These included shooting through playing cards she had tossed up in the air. Another was to shoot a metal coin tossed into the air about twenty-seven yards away. Another Oakley staple act was to look into a mirror to shoot an apple placed behind her. She was among the earliest female superstars in show business.

One demonstration that was part of Annie's routine was shooting the ashes off the tip of a large, lit cigar held in someone's mouth. The act would start with Oakley asking for a volunteer from the audience. Typically, as you can imagine, no one would volunteer, so her husband, Frank Butler, who was planted in the audience, would step forward for the exhibition.

When the Wild West Show was in Berlin, Annie made her usual request for the cigar trick. This time someone did stand up to volunteer. It was none other than the newly crowned German Emperor Kaiser Wilhelm II. Before any of his entourage could talk the emperor out of it, Kaiser Wilhelm II stood up, took out a cigar, and put it in this mouth. Annie Oakley knew quite well what she had gotten herself into. The Kaiser put the cigar in his mouth, ash at the end of it, and Oakley took aim with her Colt .45. She pulled the trigger, the shot was fired, and the ash was ripped off the cigar just a few inches in front of the Kaiser's face.

About fifteen years later, Kaiser Wilhelm II plunged the world into the mayhem of World War I. After the start of the war, Annie Oakley sent the Kaiser a letter, asking for the opportunity to take a second shot. She never received a reply.[3]

Like Annie Oakley, when it comes to our lives here on earth, we get only one shot. There are no dress rehearsals. No do-overs. No mulligans. We must take dead aim with our one shot and make it count because when this life is over, we will all face judgment (Hebrews 9:27). Though life here on earth is brief, it counts for all eternity. As Tim Chester notes, "Our life is but a moment, a breath. It's a tick of the clock. A blink of an eye. A click of the fingers. You get one life, one chance. And there's no replay, no rewind. Don't live for the moment. Live for eternity."[4]

The central thesis of this book is that every believer has one shot at life, that our one shot will one day be reviewed and rewarded by the Lord, and that our life in eternity will be dramatically affected by the result of that evaluation—that what we do now has an irreversible effect on our eternity. There are permanent repercussions for what you do, think, and say. Therefore, you must take dead aim with your life. You must maximize the one shot you have. Because what you do with that one shot will profoundly affect your life forever.

We could call this the **Reward Principle** or the **Law of Rewards.**

To state it succinctly: *The life you live today will determine your life in eternity.*

Don't let these words pass too quickly. Let this thought percolate in your mind. Let it echo in your heart. How you live, think, and act right now, every day, will reverberate in your existence forever and ever. How you do your job, love your spouse, raise your children, serve those in need, share your financial resources, love others, and overcome temptation will set the course for your existence in the endless ages to come.

The life you live today will determine your life in eternity.

We will unpack this maxim together in the chapters that follow. But before we move on, I believe it's important to briefly set forth the biblical support for the concept of future rewards for believers because many people are quick to dismiss or diminish anything to do with that.

Rewards in Focus

Most of us have probably wondered at times if our life is really amounting to much. We recognize all too well how weak and feeble our best efforts are. We ask ourselves questions like "Does what I do every day with my life really matter? Much of it seems so mundane, routine, and even inconsequential." Or, we secretly wonder, "Will God remember what I do here on earth? Will all the sacrifices I make for the Lord and others bring any reward in heaven, or is heaven the same for every believer no matter what we do on earth?"

You might even wonder if the idea of rewards is that big a deal. When the topic of future rewards comes up, it's not uncommon to hear Christians say, "Just being in heaven will be enough. That's all the reward I need. Seeing God and spending eternity with Him is reward enough. I don't care if I get anything above that or have a front row seat. Being in the back row will be enough for me as long as I'm there."

This kind of response can sound humble and pious, and it is true that being in heaven will be infinitely better than being in hell. Who could dispute that? Every believer will praise God for all eternity for making it possible to dwell in heaven with Him.

While true as far as it goes, there is also a serious shortcoming in this kind of thinking. Receiving rewards will be a sign of God's pleasure and approval of our lives here on earth. We should seek His approval above all else. Not to mention that rewards are God's idea, not ours.

> Rewards are God's doing. They were his idea, not ours. God is the one who developed the rewards, determined the criteria for awarding them, and demonstrated his grace by providing them for faithful service. Rewards arise from the heart of God...Don't rob God of the joy of being a rewarding heavenly Father because you tell him you don't care. You should care. It's okay to think about your heavenly reward. God does.[5]

The Bible commends serving God for rewards. Think about this: Jesus and the human writers of the New Testament would not have told us so much about future rewards if they didn't want us to know about them and seek them. God wants us to know that our labors and sacrifices here on earth are not in vain (1 Corinthians 15:58). He wants to motivate us when we are enduring difficult times. He wants us to know that life here counts for eternity, and that He graciously rewards sacrifice and faithfulness.

Because rewarding believers is God's idea, disregarding or denying eternal rewards is an insult to our gracious Father. The rewards God offers us are priceless treasures that He expects us to desire. "Christ offers us the incredible opportunity to trade temporary goods and currency for eternal rewards."[6] We have the opportunity now, by what we do and how we live, to assure ourselves of infinitely greater eternal rewards in the life to come.

According to the Bible, the all-knowing, all-seeing God is keeping track of how you're living and what you're doing for Him every day, and you have more to gain by living for Him than you can ever imagine. Rewards for serving Christ faithfully are beyond our wildest imagination. There will be differences among God's people in the coming kingdom and on into eternity depending on the degree of our faithfulness and sacrifice for our Lord. As Randy Alcorn notes, "Will God make all souls equal in heaven and thereby consider as equally valid a life of selfishness and indifference to others' needs as compared to a life kneeling in prayer and feeding the hungry and sharing the gospel? The Bible clearly answers no."[7]

Rewards are a big deal to God, and someday, when we stand before Him, they will be a big deal to us as well. They will be tangible evidence that we pleased the Lord with our life. For that reason, they should be important to us now, because this is the only season during which we can earn them.

Return on Investment

In order for you to see what a big deal future rewards are to God, and what a big deal they should be to you, I want to give a sampling of Scripture passages that underscore this point. There's nothing like allowing the Bible to speak for itself. You may be surprised at how much the Bible has to say about rewards. You can't read the Bible without bumping into rewards.

In the scriptural promises that follow I've italicized certain words to call attention to them. If you've never thought much about future rewards, I trust that this litany of passages will pique your interest.

> *Genesis 15:1*—"After these things the word of the LORD came to Abram in a vision, saying, "Do not fear, Abram, I am a shield to you; your *reward* shall be very great."

> *Ruth 2:12*—"May the LORD *reward* your work, and your wages be full from the LORD, the God of Israel, under whose wings you have come to seek refuge."

> *1 Samuel 24:19*—"If a man finds his enemy, will he let him go away safely? May the LORD therefore *reward* you with good in return for what you have done to me this day."

> *Psalm 19:9-11*—"The fear of the LORD is clean, enduring forever; the judgments of the LORD are true; they are righteous altogether. They are more desirable than gold, yes, than much fine gold; sweeter also than honey and the drippings of the honeycomb. Moreover, by them Your servant is warned; in keeping them there is *great reward.*"

> *Psalm 58:11*—"Men will say, 'Surely there is a *reward* for the righteous; surely there is a God who judges on earth!'"

> *Psalm 62:12*—"Lovingkindness is Yours, O Lord, for You *recompense* a man according to his work."

Proverbs 11:18—"He who sows righteousness gets a true *reward.*"

Isaiah 40:10—"Behold, the Lord GOD will come with might, with His arm ruling for Him. Behold, His *reward* is with Him and His recompense before Him."

Isaiah 62:11—"Behold, the LORD has proclaimed to the end of the earth, say to the daughter of Zion, 'Lo, your salvation comes; behold His *reward* is with Him, and His recompense before Him.'"

The theme of future rewards continues in the New Testament. The main New Testament term for rewards is the Greek word *misthos*, which occurs twenty-nine times. But there are other words that point to rewards as well, such as, *repay, inheritance, treasure,* and *crown.*

Matthew 6:3-4—"When you give to the poor, do not let your left hand know what your right hand is doing, so that your giving will be in secret; and your Father who sees *what is done* in secret will reward you."

Mathew 6:5-6—"When you pray, you are not to be like the hypocrites; for they love to stand and pray in the synagogues and on the street corners so that they may be seen by men. Truly I say to you, they have their *reward* in full. But you, when you pray, go into your inner room, close your door and pray to your Father who is in secret, and your Father who sees what is done in secret will *reward* you."

Matthew 6:16-18—"Whenever you fast, do not put on a

gloomy face as the hypocrites do, for they neglect their appearance so that they will be noticed by men when they are fasting. Truly I say to you, they have their *reward* in full. But you, when you fast, anoint your head and wash your face so that your fasting will not be noticed by men, but by your Father who is in secret; and your Father who sees what is done in secret will *reward* you."

Matthew 10:41—"He who receives a prophet in the name of a prophet shall receive a prophet's *reward*; and he who receives a righteous man in the name of a righteous man shall receive a righteous man's *reward*."

Matthew 16:27—"The Son of Man is going to come in the glory of His Father with His angels, and will then *repay* every man according to his deeds."

Matthew 19:21—"Jesus said to him, 'If you wish to be complete, go and sell your possessions and give to the poor, and you will have *treasure* in heaven; and come, follow Me.'"

Matthew 19:27-29—"Peter said to Him, 'Behold, we have left everything and followed You; what then will there be for us?' And Jesus said to them, 'Truly I say to you, that you who have followed Me, in the regeneration when the Son of Man will sit on His glorious throne, you also shall sit upon twelve thrones, judging the twelve tribes of Israel. And everyone who has left houses or brothers or sisters or father or mother or children or farms for My name's sake, will receive many times as much, and will inherit eternal life.'"

Matthew 25:19-23—"Now after a long time the master of those slaves came and settled accounts with them. The one who had received the five talents came up and brought five more talents, saying, 'Master, you entrusted five talents to me. See, I have gained five more talents.' His master said to him, 'Well done, good and faithful slave. You were faithful with a few things, I will put you in charge of many things; enter into the joy of your master.' Also the one who had received the two talents came up and said, 'Master, you entrusted two talents to me. See, I have gained two more talents.' His master said to him, 'Well done, good and faithful slave. You were faithful with a few things, I will put you in charge of many things; enter into the joy of your master.'"

Mark 9:41—"Whoever gives you a cup of water to drink because of your name as followers of Christ, truly I say to you, he will not lose his *reward*."

Luke 6:35—"Love your enemies, and do good, and lend, expecting nothing in return; and your *reward* will be great, and you will be sons of the Most High; for He Himself is kind to ungrateful and evil men."

Luke 14:12-14—"He also went on to say to the one who had invited Him, 'When you give a luncheon or a dinner, do not invite your friends or your brothers or your relatives or rich neighbors, otherwise they may also invite you in return and that will be your repayment. But when you give a reception, invite the poor, the crippled, the lame, the blind, and you will be blessed, since they do not have the means to repay you; for you will be *repaid* at the resurrection of the righteous.'"

Luke 19:15-19—"When he returned, after receiving the kingdom, he ordered that these slaves, to whom he had given the money, be called to him so that he might know what business they had done. The first appeared, saying, 'Master, your mina has made ten minas more.' And he said to him, 'Well done, good slave, because you have been faithful in a very little thing, you are to be in authority over ten cities.' The second came, saying, 'Your mina, master, has made five minas.' And he said to him also, 'And you are to be over five cities.'"

Romans 2:6—"...who will *render* to each person according to his deeds."

1 Corinthians 9:24-27—"Do you not know that those who run in a race all run, but only one receives *the prize*? Run in such a way that you may win. Everyone who competes in the games exercises self-control in all things. They then do it to receive a perishable wreath, but we an imperishable."

Ephesians 6:8—"Knowing that whatever good thing each one does, this he will receive back from the Lord, whether slave or free."

Philippians 3:13-14—"Brethren, I do not regard myself as having laid hold of it yet; but one thing I do: forgetting what lies behind and reaching forward to what lies ahead, I press on toward the goal for the *prize* of the upward call of God in Christ Jesus."

Colossians 3:22-24—"Slaves, in all things obey those who are your masters on earth, not with external service, as those who merely please men, but with sincerity of heart, fearing the Lord. Whatever you do, do your work heartily, as for the Lord rather than for men, knowing that from the Lord you will receive the *reward* of the inheritance. It is the Lord Christ whom you serve."

Hebrews 6:10—"For God is not unjust so as to forget your work and the love which you have shown toward His name, in having ministered and in still ministering to the saints."

(Notice in this verse that bestowing rewards is tied to the nature and character of God. He is just.)

Hebrews 11:6—"He who comes to God must believe that He is, and that He is a *rewarder* of those who seek Him."

Hebrews 11:25-26—"Choosing rather to endure ill-treatment with the people of God than to enjoy the passing pleasures of sin, considering the reproach of Christ greater riches than the treasures of Egypt; for he was looking to the *reward*."

1 Peter 5:4—"When the Chief Shepherd appears, you will receive the unfading *crown of glory*."

James 1:12—"Blessed is a man who perseveres under trial; for once he has been approved, he will receive the *crown of life* which the Lord has promised to those who love Him.

2 John 8—"Watch yourselves, that you do not lose what we have accomplished, but that you may receive a *full reward*."

Revelation 2:10—"Do not fear what you are about to suffer. Behold, the devil is about to cast some of you into prison, so that you will be tested, and you will have tribulation for ten days. Be faithful until death, and I will give you the *crown of life*."

Revelation 2:23—"I will *give* to each one of you according to your deeds."

Revelation 3:11—"I am coming quickly; hold fast to what you have, in order that no one take your *crown*."

Revelation 11:18—"The time came for the dead to be judged, and the time to *reward* your bond-servants the prophets and the saints and those who fear Your name, the small and the great..."

Revelation 22:12—"Behold, I am coming quickly, and My *reward* is with Me, to render to every man according to what he has done."

I hope you can see for yourself that the promise of future rewards is like a golden thread that runs through the entire Bible—from Genesis to Revelation. A time of rewards is coming. God doesn't have to reward anyone for anything. He does it because He wants to! And make no mistake: Regardless of what you and I think about it, that's exactly what He's going to do.[8]

Jesus Himself repeatedly promised rewards to the faithful as a motivation. He told them to put their treasure in heaven, where their money would be secure and yield a greater rate of return (Matthew 6:20). When Peter boldly asked Jesus about what he would receive someday in the kingdom for all his sacrifices on earth, Jesus answered with a powerful parable about God's payment of

His workers (Matthew 19:27–20:16). Jesus also taught that every believer should long to hear the words "Well done, thou good and faithful servant" (Matthew 25:21 KJV). Jesus promised His followers that if they were faithfully, sacrificially obedient, their "reward will be great" (Luke 6:35).

The problem is that the idea of serving the Lord and others to get rewards seems mercenary at best and narcissistic at worst. Should we ever serve with rewards in view? Is it ever right to do something with eternal rewards in mind?

Probably most of what we do for the Lord and others is done without any conscious thought of reward. Imagine an American soldier in Afghanistan fighting against the brutal Taliban and courageously plowing through enemy fire to rescue his fellow soldiers. Upon his return to the States, he is awarded the Congressional Medal of Honor for his heroic service. What motivated him to put his life on the line? Was it the glory of a reward? No. He harbored no thought of receiving a reward because he fully expected to die. He risked his life to save his friends' lives and defend his country's freedom. In the mountains of Afghanistan, a reward was the furthest thing from his mind. It was the givers of the award who were inspired to grant it as a way of expressing gratitude for the soldier's heroism.

In the same way, we serve God and sacrifice for Him because we love Him and others. We don't serve for the reward; we serve for the Lord. "Therefore we also have as our ambition, whether at home or absent, to be pleasing to Him" (2 Corinthians 5:9). Like a soldier receiving a medal, eternal rewards are simply God's way of showing that He is pleased with our service.

Having said that, working for rewards is biblical.

Scripture tells us Abraham was looking to his future reward: "By faith Abraham, when he was called, obeyed by going out to a place which he was to receive for an inheritance; and he went out, not knowing where he was going. By faith he lived as an alien in the land of promise, as in a foreign land, dwelling in tents with Isaac and Jacob, fellow heirs of the same promise; for he was looking for the city which has foundations, whose architect and builder is God" (Hebrews 11:8-10).

Moses had a reward mindset as well: "By faith Moses, when he had grown up, refused to be called the son of Pharaoh's daughter, choosing rather to endure ill-treatment with the people of God than to enjoy the passing pleasures of sin, considering the reproach of Christ greater riches than the treasures of Egypt; for he was looking to the reward" (Hebrews 11:24-26).

Even Jesus longed for the final reward: "Fixing our eyes on Jesus, the author and perfecter of faith, who for the joy set before Him endured the cross, despising the shame, and has sat down at the right hand of the throne of God" (Hebrews 12:2). As He faced the horror of the cross, Jesus looked to the joy set before Him in heaven.

Moses, Abraham, and the Lord Jesus are all commended because they looked beyond the immediate struggles to the reward God had in store for them. Of course, the reward to come is not the only incentive for serving Christ, but it is *a* motivating factor. Also, we also need to remember that we don't desire the reward for the reward itself, but because rewards are an expression that the way we lived is pleasing to the Lord. We ultimately desire rewards because they're a reflection of Christ's approval of us.

I hope you're beginning to see that future rewards are real. The Bible is clear that what we do now, here on earth every day, will affect our existence in the life to come, both in the coming millennium (the future 1,000-year reign of Christ on this earth) and ultimately in the new heaven and new earth for all eternity. What you do in your life now with your one shot will have repercussions that roll on forever through the endless ages.

Rewards also incentivize us to live faithfully and work tirelessly for our Lord today. The great Reformer John Calvin said, "Most assuredly, if I had merely served man, this would have been a poor recompense; but it is my happiness that I have served Him who never fails to reward His servants to the full extent of His promise."[9]

Rich Man, Poor Man

Arthur Barry is considered to be the world's greatest jewelry thief. He committed more than 150 robberies, primarily stealing jewelry, worth an estimated $5 to $10 million. He was a jewelry thief extraordinaire. He had perfected his craft and gained a twisted sense of gratification from his thievery. The only people he robbed were those whose names were on the social register. He studied his victims carefully. He robbed only the very richest. He often wore a tuxedo while committing his crimes, sometimes in broad daylight.

Arthur was finally caught and spent seventeen years in prison. After he got out, he went to work at a park at a roadside restaurant making only $50 a week. A news reporter tracked him down and interviewed him about his criminal career, and he talked freely about his life of crime.

Arthur concluded his interview this way: "I'm not very good at drawing morals, but when I was a young lad I had intelligence, charm, the ability to get along with people, and guts. I could have made something out of my life, but I didn't. So when you write the story of my life and tell about all these robberies, don't leave out the really big one. You can tell them that Arthur Barry robbed Jessie Livermore, the Wall Street baron. You can tell them that he robbed the cousin of the King of England. *But don't forget to tell them that most of all, Arthur Barry robbed Arthur Barry.*"[10]

How tragic. Arthur's greatest victim all along was himself, and he failed to see this until it was too late. The same is true for so many believers today who fail to sacrificially, consistently, and joyfully serve the Lord. They're not only robbing God, which is bad enough; they are robbing themselves at the same time. They are depriving themselves of the joy and peace that comes in this life from faithfully serving the Lord, as well as of the future rewards that will be much greater than anything we can imagine here on earth.

Where We're Headed

To help us think clearly about rewards and make sure we don't rob God or ourselves, I want to answer some key questions about final rewards in the pages that follow.

- How does the idea of receiving rewards for what we do relate to salvation without works?
- Why will God review the life of every Christian?
- Will Christians be judged for their sins?
- Will our final review be public or private?
- When will believers receive rewards?
- Where will the rewards ceremony take place?
- Will we feel sorrow and remorse at the judgment seat of Christ?
- What kinds of rewards will we get? What do we have to gain?
- What does it mean to lose reward?
- Are rewards a proper motivation for serving Christ? Is it right to serve God for rewards?
- Will every believer receive a reward?
- What if I don't have as much ability or intelligence as someone else?
- What if I came to the Lord later in life and haven't had as much time to serve Him?

These are all important questions, and the Bible addresses them.

But before we look at the answers, I would like for you to ask yourself this sobering question: What will I be doing 10,000 years from now?

Have you ever thought about that? And the fact that what you are doing today will have an effect on your life 10,000 years from now?

That's ultimately what this book is about. We should be all that we can be in this life so that we can be all that we could be in the life to come.[11]

At the beginning of this chapter I cited a brief line from a poem written by the famous missionary C.T. Studd, who poured out his life for Christ in China. Here's more of the poem. Please read these words thoughtfully and prayerfully.

> Two little lines I heard one day,
> Traveling along life's busy way;
> Bringing conviction to my heart,
> And from my mind would not depart;
> Only one life, 'twill soon be past,
> Only what's done for Christ will last.
> Only one life, yes only one,
> Soon will its fleeting hours be done;
> Then, in "that day" my Lord to meet,
> And stand before His judgment seat;
> Only one life, 'twill soon be past,
> Only what's done for Christ will last.

CHAPTER TWO

Salvation and Rewards

*Blood-washed believers will be spotless in God's sight,
but not all will have the same service record. God is after
obedience. Salvation gets us to heaven, but works
determine what we do after we get there.*

C.S. Lovett

Any discussion of rewards raises a host of questions, and we will seek to answer them in the pages that follow. But the most important issue is how good works for rewards and salvation by grace fit together. To state the issue simply: What is the relationship between faith and works, or redemption and rewards? Avoiding any confusion about these two lines of truth is essential.

We could call faith (salvation) and works the two master keys of the law or principle of rewards. Faith and works determine everything about your eternal existence and mine. Understanding what the Bible says about these truths is crucial. These two master keys are basic, yet supremely significant. Here's the simplest way I know to express these twin truths.

Key #1: Your *belief* determines *where* you will spend eternity.

Key #2: Your *behavior* determines *how* you will spend eternity.

Maintaining the proper distinction and relationship between these two keys is critical because they have to do with the heart of the truth of the gospel.

Redemption by Belief

The Bible consistently states from beginning to end that sinful people are brought into right standing with a holy God by God's grace alone through faith alone without human works. Salvation is obtained totally apart from human works, merit, or accomplishments. At least 150 times in the New Testament we are told that the sole condition for receiving eternal life is faith, belief, or trust in Jesus Christ. This truth is found as far back as the book of Genesis. Speaking of Abraham, Scripture says, "He believed in the LORD; and He reckoned it to him as righteousness" (Genesis 15:6). Righteousness was reckoned or credited to Abraham's account by his believing in the Lord. No contribution from Abraham was a part of that. He was saved by faith alone without works. Romans 4:5 says it clearly: "To the one who does not work, but believes in Him who justifies the ungodly, his faith is credited as righteousness."

In the first letter written by the apostle Paul, the epistle to the Galatians, he said explicitly, "A man is not justified by the works of the Law but through faith in Christ Jesus, even we have believed in Christ Jesus, so that we may be justified by faith in Christ and not by the works of the Law; since by the works of the Law no flesh will be justified" (Galatians 2:16). Paul's words could not be any clearer. Justification—that is, being declared righteous before God—is by faith without any works.

One of the best-known passages in the New Testament expresses the truth of salvation by grace through faith as simply as it can be stated: "By grace you have been saved through faith; and that not of yourselves, it is the gift of God; not as a result of works, so that no one may boast. For we are His workmanship, created in Christ Jesus for good works, which God prepared beforehand so that we would walk in them" (Ephesians 2:8-10).

These verses state that we are saved *by* grace *through* faith *unto* good works. The order is key: by, through, and unto. The life of good works inevitably follows salvation, but good works don't produce it or contribute to it. Good works are the fruit of salvation, not the root—the consequence, not the cause.

Titus 3:5-6 adds: "He saved us, not on the basis of deeds which we have done in righteousness, but according to His mercy, by the washing of regeneration and renewing by the Holy Spirit, whom He poured out upon us richly through Jesus Christ our Savior."

The great Bible teacher H.A. Ironside taught that when you boil it all down, there are only two religions in the world: *do* and *done*. All the religions of the world other than biblical Christianity tell us what we have to *do* to go to heaven or obtain eternal life. They all have their lists of sacred dos and don'ts. Some lists are more impressive and demanding than others, but behind them all is what a person must do to be right with God. *Do* is the watchword of man-made religion.

But not the Bible. Only the Bible tells us that everything is *done*. Scripture is clear that Jesus offered His sinless self as a perfect, once-for-all sacrifice for sin. As Jesus cried out from the cross in the darkness, "It is finished," He didn't say, "I'm finished." He said, "It is finished"—that is, the work of redemption. God has done it all. The only thing that remains for a sinful person to do is to accept the free gift of salvation God offers to all who will simply transfer their trust from self to the Savior. All we have to do is receive the pardon.

The work that saves is done forever, never to be repeated. Jesus offered one sacrifice for sins for all time, then sat down at the right hand of God (Hebrews 10:12). The picture of Jesus sitting at God's right hand conveys two beautiful truths: His work of salvation is finished, and His work of salvation has been fully accepted by the Father.

The first key to understanding the law or principle of rewards is this: Your *belief* determines *where* you will spend eternity.

Rewards by Behavior

The second key to the law of rewards is this: Your *behavior* determines *how* you will spend eternity. Works are wonderful as long as you keep them in the right place with regard to salvation:

> The biblical formula of salvation *is not* Faith + Works = Salvation
> The biblical formula of salvation *is* Faith = Salvation + Works

Good works will inevitably follow a true work of God in the heart and life of a person (James 2:12-26). Works do not bring salvation, but they confirm and validate that your faith is real and vital. As James reminds us, "Faith without works is dead" (James 2:26).

I have the great privilege of being a graduate of Dallas Theological Seminary, as well as teaching there as an associate professor in the department of Bible Exposition. I've heard that a sign used to hang outside the registrar's office for all the students to read: *Salvation is by grace...graduation is by works.*

The same could be said about the Christian life. We are saved not by our merit but by Christ's mercy. Not by our doing but by His dying. Salvation is by grace alone through faith alone in Christ alone. Yet God saved us to do good works.

As Randy Alcorn says, "We've been deceived into thinking that works is a dirty word. God condemns works done to earn salvation and works done to impress others. But our Lord enthusiastically commends works done for the right reasons."[1] As Scripture says, salvation is by grace, through faith, and for good works. "God has a lifetime of good works for each of us to do...He will reward us according to whether we do them or not."[2]

At the coming judgment seat of Christ, when you stand before the Lord, your *beliefs* won't be tested. Your *destination* for eternity won't be tested either. What will be tested are your *works*.[3] The issue of salvation is determined in this life when you trust in Jesus as your Savior from sin.

Commenting on the rewards theology of the apostle Paul, New Testament scholar Donald Guthrie fleshes out five main points: (1) God will give rewards on the basis of what a believer does in this life; (2) the rewards are partially received here, but mostly reserved in heaven; (3) the final rewards will be granted on the day of judgment; (4) the rewards are of a spiritual nature but their character is not otherwise specified; and (5) there is no suggestion that salvation itself comes under the category of reward.[4]

This chart gives a simple, visual contrast between our redemption and rewards:

Redemption	Rewards
Based on Christ's work for us	Based on our works for Christ
Received by belief	Received by behavior
Eternal destination	Eternal compensation
Past (1 John 3:2)	Future (Revelation 22:12)
Free (Ephesians 2:8-9)	Earned (1 Corinthians 3:8)
Can't be lost (John 10:28-29)	Can be lost (2 John 1:8)
Same for all Christians (Romans 3:22)	Differ among Christians (1 Corinthians 3:12-15)[5]

So, whatever else you get from this book, make sure you keep the distinction clear between these two lines of truth.

- Salvation is based on *Christ's work for us*. Rewards are based on *our works for Him*.
- Salvation comes by *belief*, rewards by *behavior*.
- Faith in Christ determines *where* we spend eternity; works for Christ determine *how* we spend eternity.

Here is another other way to state this important distinction between salvation and rewards:

- Our eternal destination (*where* we will be) is determined by our belief. Our eternal compensation (*what* we will have) is determined by our behavior.
- Redemption is provided by Christ's work for us. Rewards are procured by our works for Christ.

This is the heart of the law of rewards. The implication for our lives is undeniable and urgent. We must make sure we've trusted Jesus Christ as our Savior apart from any works whatsoever, and that after we trust Him we follow the good works He has prepared for us to do—works that please Him and secure our eternal rewards.

That's the law of rewards. This law will never be changed.

But it should change us.

CHAPTER THREE

Under Review

*The Judgment seat is meant for us
professing Christians, real and
imperfect Christians; and it tells us
that there are degrees in that
future blessedness proportioned to present faithfulness.*[1]

Alexander Maclaren

*The Bible describes the judgment seat of
Christ for one main purpose: to affect the way
we think and live—to motivate us to anticipate
with joy His return and to live our lives to please Him.*

Joe Wall

I like the story about the frustrated basketball coach, Cotton Fitzsimmons, who came up with an idea to motivate his beleaguered team. Before one game, he gave them a rousing speech that focused on the word *pretend*. "Gentlemen, when you go out there tonight, instead of remembering that we are in last place, pretend we are in first place; instead of being in a losing streak, pretend we are in a winning streak; instead of this being a regular game, pretend this is a playoff game!"[2]

With renewed inspiration, the team went onto the basketball court and was pounded by the Boston Celtics. Coach Fitzsimmons was visibly upset about the loss. But one of the star players slapped him on the back and said, "Cheer up, Coach. *Pretend* we won!"

Commenting on this story, Bible teacher Erwin Lutzer says,

> Many of us appear to be winning in the race of life, but perhaps it is all "pretend." Standing before Christ we will soon see the difference between an actual victory and wishful thinking. We will see what it took to win and what it took to lose. We'll discover that we were playing for keeps.[3]

The day is coming when every believer in Jesus Christ will stand before the Lord, and we'll discover what was pretend and what was pleasing to Him. The Bible calls this future event the judgment or *bema* seat of Christ. We will never understand what the Bible says about future rewards unless we first have a basic understanding of this event on God's prophetic calendar, so let's spend some time unpacking a few basic details about the judgment seat.

The Picture of the Judgment Seat—*What*

The first question we need to address is this: What is a judgment seat? In Scripture, the Greek word translated "judgment seat" is *bema*. The word *bema* means "to step" or "the distance a foot covers." In ancient Greek and Roman culture, the *bema* most often referred to a platform or raised stage that had steps from which judgments were handed down. This stage or platform was elevated so gathered crowds could see and hear the decisions as they were announced. A judgment seat is like the bar or raised platform upon which court judges sit in a courtroom.

The word *bema* appears in several contexts in the New Testament:

- *Bema* is used of Pilate's place of judgment (Matthew 27:19; John 19:13).
- It's used of Herod's judgment seat (Acts 12:21).
- The apostle Paul stood before the *bema* of Gallio, the proconsul of Achaia, while he was in the city of Corinth (Acts 18:12, 16-17). When you visit Corinth today, the *bema* Paul appeared before still stands on the farthest edge in the *agora* or marketplace.
- The judgment seat of Porcius Festus, before whom Paul appeared, is mentioned in Acts 26:6, 10, 17.

The term *bema* was used in three main ways in ancient Greek culture. First, it referred to a judicial tribunal where judges dispensed justice. This is the main use of *bema* in the New Testament, as you can see above.

Second, it was used of the raised platform at athletic contests in the Olympics of that day. The winning athletes received their awards at the platform.

During his second missionary journey, Paul established his ministry headquarters in Corinth for 18 months. While there, he taught the Word of God. In the city of Isthmia, a few miles from Corinth, the Isthmian Games were held every other year in the spring. Paul would certainly have visited those games while he was in Corinth working as a tentmaker and sharing the gospel. Paul's frequent use of athletic and awards imagery in his messages probably came from observing those games.

The third main use of the term *bema* was in connection with the raised stage or stand in a military camp, where medals and rewards were conferred on soldiers who exhibited heroism and bravery in battle.

Paul, inspired by the Holy Spirit, used illustrations that would help his audience to better understand the heavenly *bema* or divine tribunal at the end of the age. "For we will all stand before the judgment seat of God...So then each one of us will give an account of himself to God" (Romans 14:10, 12). "We must all appear before the judgment seat of Christ, so that each one may be recompensed for his deeds in the body, according to what he has done, whether good or bad" (2 Corinthians 5:10).

The Participants at the Judgment Seat—*Who*

Every person reading these words will appear at one of two future judgments. Both believers and unbelievers will face a final accounting. The Bible says, "Inasmuch as it is appointed for men to die once and after this comes judgment" (Hebrews 9:27). An appointment with judgment lies in the future for every person. So, the question is not "Will we be judged?" Rather, it is "When and where will we be judged?" Judgment is inescapable.

Those who have believed in Christ as Savior during this present age will appear before the judgment seat of Christ (Romans 14:10; 2 Corinthians 5:10). We might call this the *first* judgment.

Those who have rejected or neglected Christ will face the Great White Throne Judgment at the end just before the new heaven and new Earth are created. We could call this the *final* judgment.

> I saw a great white throne and Him who sat upon it, from whose presence earth and heaven fled away, and no place was found for them. And I saw the dead, the great and the small, standing before the throne, and books were opened; and another book was opened, which is the book of life; and the dead were judged from the things which were written in the books, according to their deeds. And the sea gave up the dead which were in

it, and death and Hades gave up the dead which were in them; and they were judged, every one of them according to their deeds. Then death and Hades were thrown into the lake of fire. This is the second death, the lake of fire. And if anyone's name was not found written in the book of life, he was thrown into the lake of fire.

The Great White Throne Judgment is discussed in more detail in Appendix One (pages 151-155).

Only believers in Jesus Christ will be at the judgment seat. Second Corinthians 5:10 says, "We must all appear before the judgment seat of Christ, so that each one may be recompensed for his deeds in the body, according to what he has done, whether good or bad."

The context of this passage clearly indicates that Paul was referring to himself and other believers. The word "we" refers to believers in Christ. Unbelievers will not be at this judgment.

The three words "we must all" in 2 Corinthians 5:10 tell us this judgment is all-inclusive ("we all") and mandatory ("must"). The judgment seat is not optional. It is compulsory for every believer. Attendance is required. The apostle Paul even included himself in this time of final review with the word "we." No believer is exempt. If you know Christ as your Savior you will be there.

The deacon who taught your Sunday school class will be there. The college student whose life was snuffed out by a crazed gunman at Virginia Tech University will be there. The person who led you to the Lord will be there. Paul will be there and so will Peter and John. Martin and Katherina Luther will be there. So will John and Charles Wesley. The known and the unknown. The famous and the forgotten. All who have trusted Christ as their Savior must appear before their Savior as their Judge at the judgment seat of Christ. It should be quite a company.[4]

Quite a company indeed. Make sure you're there.

The Period of the Judgment Seat—*When*

Scripture indicates that the judgment seat will take place *after* the rapture of believers to heaven but *before* the second coming of Jesus back to earth to establish His kingdom. First Corinthians 4:5 says, "Do not go on passing judgment before the time, but wait until the Lord comes who will both bring to light the things hidden in the darkness and disclose the motives of men's hearts; and then each man's praise will come to him from God." The evaluation of believers will occur when the Lord comes.

Revelation 19:7-10, which pictures the rewarded bride of Christ in heaven, supports the timing of the judgment seat of Christ between the rapture of believers to heaven and the return of Jesus to Earth. Paul Benware summarizes this timing well:

> This event apparently takes place in connection with the Rapture but prior to the Second Coming because, at the Second Coming, these believers have already been rewarded. The church has been rewarded in Revelation 19:8, where John states that "it was given to her [the church] to clothe herself in fine linen, bright and clean; for the fine linen is the righteous acts of the saints." The garments represent the rewards. The fact that the Bride is wearing her beautiful garments indicates that she has already received her rewards for her deeds of righteousness. The time of this event is clearly right before the Lord Jesus descends from heaven to conquer the world as King of kings and Lord of lords. The judgment seat of Christ, therefore, must take place prior to the Second Coming but after the church is taken to heaven by the Lord Jesus. This rewarding of believers assumes that some length of

time must be involved. And a rapture that occurs before
the final seven years allows for that needed time.[5]

Because the rewarded bride accompanies Jesus back to earth at His return (Revelation 19:14), she must have gone up to heaven some time previously. The presence of the rewarded bride in heaven prior to the second coming and her return with Jesus to Earth supports the departure of the bride to heaven at some previous time. This is also consistent with the pretribulation rapture view, which teaches that the bride of Christ will be caught up to heaven at least seven years before the second coming.[6] The seven-year period between the rapture and the return is often called the tribulation or Great Tribulation.[7] This means that believers will appear before the judgment seat in heaven while the tribulation is raging on Earth.

Another question related to the timing of the judgment seat is this: How long will it take for the Lord to review the life of every believer? If the judgment seat occurs in heaven after the rapture, will there be enough time for every believer to be evaluated by the Lord before He returns to earth at the end of the seven-year tribulation?

George Eldon Ladd says,

> It is estimated that there are two hundred million living Christians [this was written in 1956]. In seven years, there are just over two hundred million seconds. How much of a fraction of a second is necessary for the judgment of each believer? If an interval of time is needed, then far more than seven years will be required.[8]

Of course, we have no way of knowing how the Lord will judge every believer in a span of seven years, but we can rest assured that it will pose no obstacle for an unlimited God who is all-powerful and all-knowing. As John Walvoord observed, "We can infer from such judgments as that of the sheep and the goats (Matt. 25:31-46) that there is no divine problem in judging millions at once. Undoubtedly, only a fraction of the seven years between the Rapture and the Lord's return to the earth is occupied with judgments."[9]

While God's ways in carrying out the judgments may be beyond our ability to comprehend, what we do know for certain is that the judgment of believers will occur between the rapture and the second coming.

The Place of the Judgment Seat—*Where*

The judgment seat will transpire when the Lord comes (1 Corinthians 4:5). Scripture tells us that when that happens, He will take us to be with Himself in the Father's house, or heaven (John 14:1-3; 1 Thessalonians 4:17). Since the judgment seat takes place before we return with Jesus at His second advent, then this event must take place in heaven. Someday, any day—maybe even today—Jesus will come to take His bride away to heaven. When we arrive there, the first order of business will be to review and evaluate our lives. We know this will occur in heaven because the rewarded bride is pictured in heaven before she returns with Jesus back to Earth (Revelation 19:7-10).

The Principles of the Judgment Seat—*How*

Another important issue we need to consider is the *how* of the judgment seat. How will believers be judged when they stand before the Lord? The Bible reveals three facts about the way Christ will judge our lives.

Individually

Every believer will stand alone and individually before the Lord. "We will all stand before the judgment seat of God...each one of us will give an account of himself to God" (Romans 14:10, 12).

Second Corinthians 5:10 says, "We must all appear before the judgment seat of Christ, so that each one may be recompensed for his deeds in the body, according to what he has done, whether good or bad." Notice in this verse how Paul moved from the plural "we" to the singular "each one...his...he." Each one of us will have to sing solo before the Lord.

Erwin Lutzer captures something of the drama of this scene:

> Imagine staring into the face of Christ. Just the two of you, one-on-one! Your entire life is present before you. In a flash you see what He sees. No hiding. No opportunity to put a better spin on what you did. No attorney to represent you. The look in His eyes says it all. Like it or not, that is precisely where you and I shall be someday.[10]

Impartially

The Lord is no respecter of persons. "There is no partiality with God" (Romans 2:11). "He who does wrong will receive the consequences of the wrong which he has done, and that without partiality" (Colossians 3:25). God is a fair judge. At the judgment seat, the rich, wealthy, and beautiful won't be able to get a better deal or purchase rewards. God is impartial. Everyone will get a fair shake.

Everyone will be judged by the same standard. However, there is one group that will be judged by a more stringent standard—those who teach God's Word and lead the Lord's people. James 3:1 says, "Let not many of you become teachers, my brethren, knowing that as such we will incur a stricter judgment" (see also Hebrews 13:17). I once heard someone say, "If you are standing in line at the judgment seat and you see a line with a bunch of preachers in it, get in another line. It will go faster." That's true. Those who teach God's Word will be held to a higher standard and will be judged in two main areas: (1) Was your teaching accurate? and (2) Did you live it out in your own life?

Jesus said, "Whoever then annuls one of the least of these commandments, and teaches others to do the same, shall be called least in the kingdom of heaven; but whoever keeps and teaches them, he shall be called great in the kingdom of heaven" (Matthew 5:19). Notice that Jesus said whoever "keeps and teaches" God's Word will be called great in the kingdom. This is a sobering challenge for all who handle God's Word before others. Every Bible teacher and pastor should take these sobering words to heart.

Because the Lord is impartial, He will take into account how long we have been saved as well as the opportunities, resources, and abilities He has placed at our disposal (Matthew 20:1-16). We'll look at these specifics in greater detail in chapter 9.

Inclusively

Our accounting at the judgment seat will also be all-encompassing. The divine Inspector won't miss a thing. His judgment will be thorough, including both *what* we did (our actions) and *why* we did it (our motives). When it comes to rewards, the Bible is clear that God is just as concerned about the *why* of our service as the *what* or *how*. Nothing will escape the scrutinizing eye of the Savior. "There is no creature hidden from His sight, but all things are open and laid bare to the eyes of Him with whom we have to do" (Hebrews 4:13).

The Heidelberg Catechism Q&A 91 highlights the importance of motive in our works for the Lord.

> Q. What are good works?
>
> A. Only those which are done out of true faith, conform to God's law, and are done for God's glory; and not those based on our own opinion or human tradition.

This catechism underscores an important point: For works to be good, they must be done for God's glory.

That motives matter at the judgment seat is clear. "Do not go on passing judgment before the time, but wait until the Lord comes who will both bring to light the things hidden in the darkness and disclose the motives of men's hearts; and then each man's praise will come to him from God" (1 Corinthians 4:5).

There are many corrupt motives that can taint our actions. We may serve God and others for personal gain, and we may serve from a spirit of self-promotion and pride. In everything we do, Jesus knows our motive. He knows why we do what we do.

I like the story about the burglar who broke into a house late one night. He thought no one was home. As he tiptoed through the living room, he froze when he heard a loud voice say, "Jesus is watching you!" After silence returned, the burglar crept forward again. "Jesus is watching you!" the voice boomed again.

The burglar stopped dead in his tracks. He was frightened. Frantically, he looked all around. In a dark corner he spotted a bird cage, and in the cage was a parrot. He asked the parrot, "Was that you who said Jesus is watching me?"

"Yes," said the parrot.

The burglar breathed a sigh of relief. Then he asked, "What's your name?"

"Moses," said the bird.

"That's a dumb name for a parrot," sneered the burglar. "What idiot named you Moses?"

The parrot responded, "The same idiot who named the Rottweiller *Jesus*. Sic 'em, Jesus!"

The parrot was right—Jesus is watching you! And He's watching me. He sees us. He knows us.

God doesn't judge the book of our life by its cover; He reads the pages and the footnotes.

The word "appears" in 2 Corinthians 5:10 means much more

than just showing up at the judgment seat. It means "to be made manifest." The Lord will turn us inside out at the judgment seat. Every hidden motive, thought, and deed we have done in Christ's service will be exposed.

We will be fully disclosed at the *bema* seat. The Lord will know the motives of our hearts. First Corinthians 4:5 is very clear: "The Lord...will both bring to light the things hidden in the darkness and disclose the motives of men's hearts; and then each man's praise will come to him from God."

Jesus highlighted the importance of our motives in the giving of rewards.

> Beware of practicing your righteousness before men to be noticed by them; otherwise you have no reward with your Father who is in heaven. So when you give to the poor, do not sound a trumpet before you, as the hypocrites do in the synagogues and in the streets, so that they may be honored by men. Truly I say to you, they have their reward in full...When you pray, you are not to be like the hypocrites; for they love to stand and pray in the synagogues and on the street corners so that they may be seen by men. Truly I say to you, they have their reward in full...Whenever you fast, do not put on a gloomy face as the hypocrites do, for they neglect their appearance so that they will be noticed by men when they are fasting. Truly I say to you, they have their reward in full (Matthew 6:1-2, 5, 16).

The words "have...in full" were repeated three times by Jesus. They translate a Greek term that means "to be paid in full," "to receive a receipt for full payment." Jesus was saying that if we serve God to receive praise and notoriety from others, we had better enjoy whatever accolades we get because that is all we will ever know. Jesus will judge our motives. He sees everything clearly.

At the judgment seat, the conduct, service, and motives of every believer will be turned inside out and will appear in their true light. We can often fool other people about our service and motives and lead them to think we are doing some great things for God. But we can't fool God Himself. He knows what we do and why we do it, and His reward will be based on the true estimation of our actions and attitudes. Many whom we assume will receive great rewards in heaven may walk away with very little, and vice versa. We would do well to remember the words Jesus spoke in Matthew 20:16: "The last shall be first, and the first last."

God sees *to us*, and He sees *through us*. No one will be able to claim that they received less than they should have, or that God overlooked anything. The judgment will be thorough and comprehensive.

The Purpose of the Judgment Seat—Why

The purpose of the judgment seat of Christ is *not* to determine whether people will enter heaven or hell, or to mete out punishment for sin. A person's eternal destiny was already decided when he or she believed in Jesus Christ as their Savior from sin. The issue of where we will spend eternity won't even come up. God's Word clearly states that His children will never be judged for their sins. Jesus said, "Truly, truly, I say to you, he who hears My word, and believes Him who sent Me, has eternal life, and does not come into judgment, but has passed out of death into life" (John 5:24). Paul wrote, "There is now no condemnation for those who are in Christ Jesus" (Romans 8:1). In Scripture our sins are pictured as pardoned, forgiven, blotted out, and cast into the depths of the sea. The Bible is clear that believers will never *suffer* for their sins, but will we *see* our sins at the judgment seat?

Theologian Anthony Hoekema maintains that the answer is yes. He asks, "How can any deeds of believers be brought into the open without some recognition of sin and imperfections?" He then adds this qualifier: "But—and this is the important point—the sins and shortcomings of believers will be revealed in the judgment as *forgiven sins*, whose guilt has been totally covered by the blood of Jesus Christ. Therefore...believers have nothing to fear from the judgment."[11]

I don't believe we will see our sins at the judgment seat, even as forgiven sins. But either way, the Bible is clear that we will not face judgment for our sins. If even one sin could ever be brought against one of God's children, then Christ's work was incomplete. Our salvation rests wholly on the person and work of Christ in our place. The issue at the judgment seat is not salvation, but rewards. Salvation comes through Christ's work for us (Ephesians 2:8-9). Rewards are based on our works for Christ.

To put it another way, the purpose of the judgment seat *is not* to condemn us but to commend us—not to punish us but to praise us. Simply stated, the object of the judgment seat is to review and to reward. "Faithfulness will be graciously rewarded while unfaithfulness will go unrewarded. Thus the primary purpose of the judgment seat of Christ is to reveal and review the Christian's life and service and then to reward him for what God deems worthy of reward."[12]

There's a cynical statement that says, "No good deed goes unpunished." With the Lord, the opposite is true: "No good deed goes unrewarded." The all-knowing, all-seeing Lord will review us and reward us accordingly. "Each man's work will become evident; for the day will show it because it is to be revealed with fire, and the fire itself will test the quality of each man's work" (1 Corinthians 3:13).

Jesus will examine and evaluate our faithfulness in light of the abilities and opportunities God has given us. I've heard it said that our works—good and bad—are like tin cans tied to a dog's tail. We can't get away from them. We can't shake them. They will follow us to the *bema* seat of Christ.

Second Corinthians 5:10 refers to the works of believers as either "good or bad." We know what the "good" works are, but what are the "bad"? The Greek word translated "bad" is *phaulos*, which means "bad" in the sense of worthless, not in the sense of evil. As we have already seen, the issue at the judgment seat will not be our sins. Those were paid for at the cross. So, if these bad works aren't sin, then what are they? They are what we might call "bad" good works. What makes these bad or worthless is that they are performed with the wrong motive. That's why these works are not worthy of reward. They are nonrewardable deeds because they are done for the wrong reason. They correspond to the "wood, hay, straw" in 1 Corinthians 3:12. The bad works that will be reviewed at the judgment seat are right actions done the wrong way. Our hands and heart must go together.

At the judgment seat, this old saying will be proven true: "One day we must all sit down at the banquet of consequences."

Flyover Faithfulness

Oscar Hammerstein, the famous composer, told a story about the time "he saw a picture of the top of the head of the Statue of Liberty, taken from a helicopter."[13] Hammerstein was stunned by the amount of detail and painstaking effort that was put into the lady's coiffure. It occurred to Hammerstein that the sculptor could have never imagined, even in his wildest dreams, that people would one day be able to fly over the statue and look down on a rather hidden part of his creation. Nevertheless, he gave as much attention to detail at the top of the head as he did to the face, arms, and legs. In his book *Lyrics*, he wrote, "When you are creating a work of art, or any other kind of work, finish the job off perfectly. You never know when a helicopter, or some other instrument not at the moment invented may come along and find you out."[14]

The Lord doesn't need a helicopter. He sees it all—the big and the small, the hidden and the unseen things we can hide from others.

God is watching. He's keeping track. Nothing is veiled from His sight (Hebrews 4:13). He looks down every day on what we do, think, and say. Therefore, we must do our best work for Him as we are empowered by the Spirit at all times.

Others may never see the painstaking work and detail of our efforts, but God knows, and one day our diligence will come to light. He will reward us for every act of faithfulness done for Him, no matter how small, "right down to every cup of cold water we give to the needy in His name" (Mark 9:41).[15]

CHAPTER FOUR

Your Dream House

*We should be all that we can be on earth so
that we can be all that we could be in heaven.*[1]

Erwin Lutzer

The New Testament uses several vivid images to describe our future judgment and reward before the Lord: a disciplined athlete (1 Corinthians 9:24-27), a faithful steward overseeing the resources of another person (4:1-5), and a careful builder (3:10-15). These are common illustrations every person can understand. The portrayal of our life as a homebuilding project that the Lord will inspect someday certainly strikes a chord with many in our culture today. It's hard to imagine that there's ever been a time in history when people have known more about building and buying a home than today. In the last few years some of the most popular shows on TV are about building, renovating, and flipping houses, as well as locating the perfect home. Here are just a few examples.

- *Flip or Flop*
- *Property Brothers*

- *This Old House*
- *Fixer Upper*
- *Love It or List It*
- *House Hunter*

The primary appeal of these programs is that every family needs a place to live. We love our homes. The largest investment most people make is their house. Home is where we spend most of our time and create lasting memories.

Scripture pictures our life as a home construction project that the Lord will inspect someday. The question for every believer is not *whether* we are constructing a building—all of us are doing that. Rather, it is this: What kind of material are we using? Every believer is building for as long as he or she lives.

> We are God's fellow workers; you are God's field, God's building. According to the grace of God which was given to me, like a wise master builder I laid a foundation, and another is building on it. But each man must be careful how he builds on it. For no man can lay a foundation other than the one which is laid, which is Jesus Christ. Now if any man builds on the foundation with gold, silver, precious stones, wood, hay, straw, each man's work will become evident; for the day will show it because it is to be revealed with fire, and the fire itself will test the quality of each man's work. If any man's work which he has built on it remains, he will receive a reward. If any man's work is burned up, he will suffer loss; but he himself will be saved, yet so as through fire (1 Corinthians 3:10-15).[2]

Every believer in Christ is a builder constructing a house. Someday the divine building inspector will come to evaluate how we've constructed our dwelling. Our work will be tested with fire. Only that which remains will bring rewards to us.

As is true with any building, the foundation is what matters most in our lives. It determines our destiny. The only foundation that can stand in the end is the solid rock of Jesus Christ (Matthew 7:24-25). He alone will never change or be destroyed. He is the only foundation that is secure. However, the superstructure we build on top of the foundation determines our rewards. That's what the Lord will review at the judgment seat. The issue at the judgment seat won't be our *position* before the Lord, but our *performance* for Him.

In October 2018, Hurricane Michael slammed the Florida Gulf Coast with brute force. One of the hardest hit areas was Mexico Beach. The photographs and video of the devastation in the hurricane's wake were stunning. Buildings were flattened. Homes were scraped off their foundations. The area looked like a war zone. However, one house, known as the Sand Palace, was still standing surrounded by rubble. I heard the owner of the house, Dr. Lebron Lackey, interviewed on Fox News about how his home was able to withstand the onslaught. He said the building codes required that structures be able to withstand winds ups to 125-150 mph. He built his house to withstand winds of 250 mph.

He said the reason his house stood is found 40 feet below the surface. The code called for pilings 30 feet deep, but he put his 40 feet down. That applies to us as well. If we want to stand against the winds and storms of this life, it's not going to be on account of what's visible on the outside. Our strength will come from what is hidden down under the surface in our foundation, Jesus Christ. He undergirds, supports, and sustains all we do. Our life must be built on Him so that we can stand strong.

Gold Standard

As we construct our spiritual house on the foundation of Jesus Christ, we decide each day which materials we will use. We can select from two basic categories: wood, hay, and straw, or gold, silver, and precious stones. We all know that wood, hay, and straw are highly combustible, don't last long, and are not sturdy—just ask the three little pigs. These cheaper materials are easier to build with, take less time, and may be attractive, but they won't stand the test of fire. When Jesus comes, those who have used these inferior materials will find their superstructure reduced to ashes.

Gold, silver, and precious stones, on the other hand, are valuable, enduring, high quality materials. They are smaller in size, more difficult to obtain, more valuable, and most importantly, able to survive the fire.[3] What are the gold, silver, and precious stones that we should use to build our lives? Some examples of these materials are truth, love, integrity, purity, and sacrificial service. To sum up these lasting building elements, we could say they are Christlike qualities in our lives. "If Christ is the foundation of our lives, He should be the center of the work we build on the foundation."[4] We build with our conduct, our service, and our motives. Anything in our lives that reflects the character of Jesus will last and remain.

A few years ago, my wife Cheryl and I (mainly Cheryl) built a new house. We had a fun time together purchasing our lot and deciding on a plan. Cheryl was there almost every day overseeing the construction work. She spent countless hours picking out tile, fixtures, paint, brick, appliances, and carpet. We had to make numerous choices about the cost and quality of the materials to build our home. We did our best to choose that which was high quality and reliable. We wanted our house to last.

You're building a house too. Choose the best-quality materials. The fire test is coming.

Blueprints First

To know what kind of materials to use in your spiritual building project, you must consult the biblical blueprint. Scripture lays out the plans for how to build a life that will stand the test of time and pass the final inspection. If you follow its precepts, priorities, and purposes, your life-construction project will be successful. You need to consult God's Word regularly to know how to build a life with lasting results.

Addison Mizner found fame and fortune during the early part of the twentieth century as chief architect to the moneyed elite during south Florida's property boom. He used a very unorthodox, scattered method that often produced unexpected results. In one house, for example, he overlooked a rather significant detail: a staircase connecting the first and second stories. After completing the work of constructing Baltimore's Howard Hotel, the contractors installed boilers, started fires, and quickly discovered that Mizner had forgotten to build a chimney.

When William Gray Warden excitedly asked Mizner to get a copy of the blueprints for his future Palm Beach home, Mizner replied that they were unavailable. Warden asked why he didn't have them, and Mizner famously replied, "Why, the house isn't built yet! Construction first, blueprints afterward."

That's a terrible way to build a *house*, but an even worse way to build a *life*.

Yet that's what we see happening all around us today. People are building their lives without consulting the divine blueprints. They're following their own desires, opinions, taste, and choices. It's "construction first, blueprints afterward." We see the chaos that results from this kind of construction all around us in our culture. Families are falling apart, and the moral and social fabric of our society is unraveling.

Are you following the divine blueprint for your life? Are you building your house according to the biblical plan?

Your House

I like the story of the building contractor who was asked by his rich friend to build him a house. While doing the project, the contractor frequently cut corners to line his own pockets. He skimped on quality in certain places, such as the foundation and framing, knowing that the problems wouldn't become manifest for years. On the surface the house looked great, but within, the quality and workmanship was poor.

You can imagine the deep regret and disappointment the contractor felt when he finished the house and his rich friend handed him the keys to the house as a gift, with just one condition: that he live in the house for the rest of his life!

This reckless builder thought he was shortchanging his rich friend, but he ended up robbing himself. The same can be true of us. Our shoddy, selfish service not only robs the Lord of His glory but robs us of rewards the Lord wants us to enjoy.[5]

One of the strangest houses in America is known as the Winchester House in San Jose, California. It was built by Sarah Winchester, who inherited $20 million from her husband, who made his wealth producing the famous Winchester rifles. Her only daughter died a mere five weeks after birth, and out of grief, or possibly guilt, Sarah became obsessed with the occult. She embarked on an epic building project after being told by a medium that as long as she continued to add on to her house, she would not die.

The original structure was an eight-room farmhouse. She hired sixteen carpenters and put them to work. For the next thirty-eight years, the craftsmen labored every day, twenty-four hours a day, to build a mansion. Observers were intrigued by the project. Sarah's instructions were more than eccentric; they were eerie. The design has a macabre feel. Each window was to have thirteen panes, each wall thirteen panels, each closet thirteen hooks, and each chandelier thirteen globes.

All through the house are mindless twists and turns. Corridors snake randomly, some leading nowhere. One door opens to a blank wall, another to a fifty-foot drop. One set of stairs leads to a ceiling that has no door. There are trap doors, secret passageways, and tunnels.

The completed estate sprawls over 6 acres and has 6 kitchens, 13 bathrooms, 40 stairways, 47 fireplaces, 52 skylights, 467 doors, 10,000 windows, and a bell tower.

The making of this mysterious mansion ended when Sarah died. After her death, it took eight trucks working full-time for over a period of forty days to haul away all the leftover building materials and junk.

Like Sarah Winchester, each of us is building a house. When we die, our project will be finished. When the Lord calls us home to heaven, our handiwork will be inspected. The question for each of us is this: What kind of house are we building? Will it stand in the final day?

Are you building a house with stairways to nowhere, random skylights, pointless doors, unnecessary tunnels, and rooms with no purpose?

Or are you building a lasting, rewardable life on the solid foundation of Jesus Christ?

CHAPTER FIVE

A Rewarding Q & A

*The small will be great. The forgotten will be
remembered. The unnoticed will be crowned, and
the faithful will be honored... Your day is coming.
What the world has overlooked, your Father has remembered,
and sooner than you can imagine, you will be blessed by him.*[1]

Max Lucado

Like the subjects of heaven and the afterlife in general, the topics of eternal rewards and the judgment seat of Christ raise many questions. When we think about the future earthly kingdom of Christ and the eternal heaven, many of us have more questions than answers. That's why books about people claiming to have died, visited heaven, and come back have filled the bestseller lists for years. Everyone has questions about heaven. Some of those questions may have motivated you to buy this book and read it.

While I certainly don't claim to have all the answers or even know all the relevant questions, I want to do my best in this chapter to attempt to answer some of the key questions many people ask about heavenly rewards.

Key Questions About Heavenly Rewards

What will happen immediately after the judgment seat?

While there is disagreement on the timing of the rapture of believers to heaven, I believe the rapture will occur before the seven-year time of tribulation. This is called the pretribulation rapture view and maintains the rapture is the next event on God's prophetic calendar. After the bride of Christ arrives in heaven, the very first event is the judgment seat of Christ, which will be followed by the marriage of the Lamb, which is the marriage of the church or bride of Christ to her Bridegroom, the Lord Jesus.

> "Let us rejoice and be glad and give the glory to Him, for the marriage of the Lamb has come and His bride has made herself ready." It was given to her to clothe herself in fine linen, bright and clean; for the fine linen is the righteous acts of the saints. Then he said to me, "Write, 'Blessed are those who are invited to the marriage supper of the Lamb'" (Revelation 19:7-10).

Notice that the bride in heaven is clothed in fine linen, which represents "the righteous acts of the saints." This language presupposes that the bride has been rewarded.

We can apply this scenario to our daily lives. Many a prospective bride is consumed with her wedding day. She thinks about what she is going to wear at her wedding and the reception afterward. She spends countless hours, days, and months carefully shopping for her dress, shoes, veil, jewelry, and all the accessories. Then when the wedding day finally arrives, there are many more final preparations: a manicure, a pedicure, hair styling, and makeup. Nothing is overlooked; no detail is left to chance.

Our preparation for the marriage of the Lamb should be no different. As we just noticed, Revelation 19:8 says we will be present at the wedding feast dressed in white linen, or our righteous deeds. These good deeds are not works we've done to enter heaven—we cannot earn the garments of righteousness that Christ has provided for us by His death on the cross. However, we are to make ourselves ready for the wedding feast by sewing the garment we will wear for the occasion. How we are dressed on the day we are presented to Christ will depend on the life we have lived for Christ in this life.

At the marriage of the bride to the Lamb, each of us will be wearing the wedding garment of our own making. That's an arresting yet exciting thought. Our desire should be to make sure we are beautifully adorned on that future day, and that will depend on how we are living for Christ in the here and now. The marriage of the Lamb is coming. Someday the Bridegroom will come to take His bride to His Father's house.

Are you living a righteous life for your loving Bridegroom so that your garment will be bright and beautiful?

What does it mean to lose rewards?

The Bible is clear that rewards can be lost or forfeited. "Watch yourselves, that you do not lose what we have accomplished, but that you may receive a full reward" (2 John 8). D.M. Panton notes, "That a crown may be lost to a believer is as certain as any truth in the Holy Scripture."[2]

Once again, we must remember that while rewards can be lost, salvation can never be forfeited (John 10:27-30; Romans 8:28-30, 35-39; Philippians 1:6). Eternal life is not fifty or one hundred years in duration. Eternal life is eternal—it can never be lost. Every believer is a child of God. We can be disinherited of rewards, but we can never be "de-sonned."

Gaining eternal rewards will bring indescribable joy to us, which means that losing rewards is serious. According to Scripture, rewards can be lost in three main ways: by default, defect, or disqualification.

Loss by Default

Rewards can be taken or snatched by someone else not through theft, but by defaulting on or shirking our responsibility. Rewards can also be lost by defaulting them to someone else. In Revelation 3:11 Jesus said, "I am coming quickly; hold fast what you have, so that no one will take your crown." Woodrow Kroll observes:

> We should never conceive of the loss of rewards as a repossession. God does not take back something he has already awarded to us. At the heavenly bema, we do not suddenly have a quantity of rewards ripped from our hands by the righteous Judge. We are not stripped of rewards as an erring soldier is stripped of his stripes. Not at all...Loss or reward is not like handing back a trophy that was mistakenly given to you. It's not returning something you earned. It's forfeiting a reward that you could have earned but failed to do so.[3]

I read the following words from H.A. Ironside years ago, and it had quite an impact on my thinking about serving the Lord and losing rewards by default:

> No one can rob me of my salvation. Of this there is abundant evidence in Scripture. But another may take my crown if I prove faithless to the trust committed to me...If I do not exercise the ministry allotted to me, in humble dependence on the Holy Spirit that I may fulfill it faithfully, I may be set aside as a servant, and another may be called to complete my work. And so I will lose my crown.
>
> We have read of the tract distributor who, becoming discouraged because of apparent lack of appreciation, gave up his lowly service, and learned twenty years after of

one saved through a tract given out the last day in which he did the work, who had taken it up himself as a ministry to needy men and after that long lapse of time met his benefactor and presented him with a tract. As a result a conversation sprang up which showed how the convert had taken the other's place, and the older man exclaimed with regret, "I see: I have let you take my crown.[4]

No one can steal your crown, but you can lose your heavenly rewards by default—by failing to seize the opportunities presented to you.

Loss by Defect

Losing a reward by defect means that our service is defective or deficient in some way. This happens when we choose inferior materials to build our lives and do the Lord's work. If we choose what is expedient, easy, and ephemeral we forfeit our Lord's approval. We could compare this to a mechanic or repairman using shoddy parts to make a repair. The work is defective.

Our work can also be defective when our motives are wrong. As we've already seen, God cares about the *why* as well as the *what*. Self-promoting motives render our works defective, resulting in loss of rewards.

Loss by Disqualification

One of the most sobering passages on the reality and danger of loss of reward was written by the apostle Paul:

> Do you not know that those who run in a race all run, but only one receives the prize? Run in such a way that you may win. Everyone who competes in the games exercises self-control in all things. They then do it to receive a perishable wreath, but we an imperishable. Therefore

> I run in such a way, as not without aim; I box in such a
> way, as not beating the air; but I discipline my body and
> make it my slave, so that, after I have preached to oth-
> ers, I myself will not be *disqualified* (1 Corinthians 9:24-
> 27, emphasis added).

As we saw earlier, the background for this passage is the ancient Isthmian Games in which athletes competed for prizes. The word "disqualified" is a translation of the Greek word *adokimos*, which means "declared unfit" or "rejected." In this context it refers to being disqualified or denied participation in an athletic event. When an athlete broke the rules, he was prohibited from taking part. Similar imagery was employed by Paul in 2 Timothy 2:5: "If anyone competes as an athlete, he does not win the prize unless he competes according to the rules." For Christians, the rules are found in God's Word. Disqualification comes from failing to keep the instructions set forth in God's Word.

Again, we must always remember that the point of these texts is not loss of salvation, but disqualification for rewards. No matter what happens to us in terms of rewards, it will not affect our redemption.

Everyone knows that the only way an athlete can win is by competing. So disqualification means being eliminated from any opportunity to receive the prize. The modern-day equivalent is a player getting benched by a coach or suspended from participation. You can't help the team win if you're not in the game.

When Paul warned about the danger of disqualification, he included himself in the warning. He knew that even as an apostle he had to discipline himself to maximize his opportunities for receiving the prize. If someone as great as the apostle Paul was genuinely concerned about the possibility of being benched, we must take seriously the need for us to be well-disciplined.

Not long before his death, Paul made it clear that he had not been disqualified by the Lord. "In the future there is laid up for me the crown of righteousness, which the Lord, the righteous Judge, will award to me on that day; and not only to me, but also to all who have loved His appearing" (2 Timothy 2:8). Paul was faithful to the end, staying the course. May each of us have the same hope and confidence when the end of our life draws near.

What are some of the specific ways we can be disqualified? In the verses right after 1 Corinthians 9:27, Paul pointed to the wilderness generation in Exodus as a tragic example of disqualification. They're Exhibit *A* of those who failed to win the prize.

> Now these things happened as examples for us, so that we would not crave evil things as they also craved. Do not be idolaters, as some of them were; as it is written, "The people sat down to eat and drink, and stood up to play." Nor let us act immorally, as some of them did, and twenty-three thousand fell in one day. Nor let us try the Lord, as some of them did, and were destroyed by the serpents. Nor grumble, as some of them did, and were destroyed by the destroyer. Now these things happened to them as an example, and they were written for our instruction, upon whom the ends of the ages have come (1 Corinthians 10:6-11).

Four specific disqualifying sins are underscored in these verses: (1) idolatry, (2) sexual immorality, (3) trying or challenging the Lord, and (4) grumbling. We might be surprised to see grumbling or complaining in this list, but the wilderness generation turned grumbling into an Olympic sport. At least ten major instances of their complaining are recorded in Exodus and Numbers. Grumbling is a serious spiritual malady that manifests a heart of ingratitude. Make no mistake—a grousing, grumbling, griping spirit will get you benched. The danger of disqualification is real. The Exodus generation never made it to their reward, the land of promise.

They persisted in unbelief and disobedience, and that resulted in their disqualification. Believers today face the same kind of danger."[5]

Knowing that rewards can be lost or squandered—and that we can get benched—should cause each of us to make sure we maximize our gains and minimize our losses by carefully following the rules of life God has graciously given to us in His Word.

How long will rewards last?

Believers will receive their rewards at the judgment seat of Christ in heaven before returning to Earth with Jesus at His second advent. Then we will enjoy and employ the benefits of these rewards during the 1,000-year earthly reign of Christ, during which we will reign with Him (Revelation 20:1-6). After the millennial reign is over, God will create a new heaven and new Earth (Revelation 21:1-8). At that time, this present heaven and Earth or universe will be destroyed by God and recreated. The new heaven and new Earth won't be a renovation or remodel of the old universe, but an entirely new creation. The heavenly city, the New Jerusalem, will come down and sit on the new Earth as the capital city of the new universe.

Rewards will last not just for the millennial kingdom, but for all eternity. Nothing in Scripture suggests that the rewards received at the judgment seat will be set aside at the end of the millennium, so we can safely assume the rewards and the ruling will last forever (Revelation 22:5).

Will every believer receive a reward?

After laboring for months writing *The French Revolution*, Thomas Carlyle took his manuscript to his friend John Stuart Mill for his evaluation. Mill passed the manuscript on to a woman named Mrs. Chapman, who read it by a fireplace on the evening of March 5, 1834. Before retiring to bed, she laid the manuscript on the mantel.

Early the next morning, a servant girl came to clean the room and start a fire in the fireplace. Not knowing what the papers were, she used the manuscript to kindle a fire. Months of tedious work was burned up in a matter of seconds.[6]

That's how it will be for many at the judgment seat. Years of life and labor will go up in flames because they were done for the wrong reason. Many will face the ashes of a worthless, wasted life. But does this mean that some believers will receive no reward at all? For some Christians, will everything go up in smoke? Will there be some who, at the judgment seat of Christ, will walk away emptyhanded?

For many years when I taught about the judgment seat of Christ, I taught that perspective—that some believers will receive no reward. To support that view I would quote 1 Corinthians 3:13-15: "Each man's work will become evident; for the day will show it because it is to be revealed with fire, and the fire itself will test the quality of each man's work. If any man's work which he has built on it remains, he will receive a reward. If any man's work is burned up, he will suffer loss; but he himself will be saved, yet so as through fire."

I taught that some believers will make it through the fire with nothing but their life. They can't lose their salvation, so it's not at stake, but they will lose everything else. Based on 1 Corinthians 3:15, I once heard the well-known Bible teacher J. Vernon McGee say something to the effect that at the judgment seat, some believers will smell like they were bought at a fire sale.

Here's a powerful poem that expresses the idea that some believers will go unrewarded:

> When I stand at the judgment seat of Christ
> And He shows me His plan for me;
> The plan of my life as it might have been
> Had He had His way, and I see
> How I blocked Him here and I checked Him there
> And I would not yield my will,
> Shall I see grief in my Savior's eyes;
> Grief though He loves me still

Oh, He'd have me rich, and I stand there poor,
Stripped of all but His grace,
While my memory runs like a hunted thing
Down the paths I can't retrace.
Then my desolate heart will well-nigh break
With tears that I cannot shed.
I'll cover my face with my empty hands
And bow my uncrowned head.

No. Lord of the years that are left to me
I yield them to Thy hand.
Take me, make me, mold me
To the pattern Thou hast planned.[7]

Martha Snell Nicholson

Several years ago I changed my opinion about this based on the words of 1 Corinthians 4:5: "Do not go on passing judgment before the time, but wait until the Lord comes who will both bring to light the things hidden in the darkness and disclose the motives of men's hearts; and then each man's praise will come to him from God."

The words "*each man's* praise will come to him from God" (emphasis added) indicate that every person will receive some kind of reward. Each man includes every believer. Jesus will find something to reward to every one of us. Knowing this should excite and encourage us. Referring to the words "each man's praise will come to him from God" in 1 Corinthians 4:5, Max Lucado says,

What an incredible sentence. God will praise each one of them. Not the "best of them" nor a "few of them" nor "the achievers among them," but "God will praise each one of them." You won't be left out. God will see to that. In fact, God himself will give the praise. When it comes to giving recognition, God does not delegate the job.

Michael doesn't hand out the crowns. Gabriel doesn't speak on behalf of the throne. God himself does the honors. God himself will praise his children.[8]

Randy Alcorn adds:

> God will reward the child who gave to the missions offering the money she'd saved for a softball mitt. He'll reward the teenager who kept himself pure despite all the temptations. He'll reward the man who tenderly cared for his wife with Alzheimer's, the mother who raised the child with cerebral palsy, the child who rejoiced despite his handicap. He'll reward the parent who modeled Christ to their children and the children who followed him despite their parents' bad example. He'll reward those who suffered while trusting him, and those who hold the ones who were suffering. He'll reward the couple who downsized, selling their large house to live in a small one to give all the money away to missions.[9]

Always remember: Any reward we get will be purely due to the grace of God. And Scriptures give us hope and reassurance that our Lord, in His grace, *will* reward us. Stop and think about that for a moment: The Lord of the ages, the Creator of the universe, the Shepherd of the stars will praise you and me if we have placed our trust in Christ.

Will we feel remorse and shame at the judgment seat of Christ?

At the judgment seat, there's no getting around the fact that we will all feel some sense of loss and shame. There will certainly be tears. How can we fail to experience regret and remorse as many of our works go up in flames (1 Corinthians 3:15), and we see how our actions disqualified us from receiving the prize (1 Corinthians 9:27)?

Reflecting on how we lived and the opportunities we squandered will surely result in some amount of regret, especially in light of the great price Jesus paid for our forgiveness. The apostle John warned us about remorse in heaven: "Now, little children, abide in Him, so that when He appears, we may have confidence and not shrink away from Him in shame at His coming" (1 John 2:28). Referring to this verse and the shame at His coming, Dr. Mark Bailey says, "The grammar of this passage suggests the self-realizing embarrassment of shame at the appearing of the Lord rather than any punitive shaming from the Lord. Believers will not be condemned."[10]

Without negating the reality of celestial tears and self-realized shame, I believe the primary purpose of the judgment seat is not loss but gain, not defeat but victory. Loss will be present and real, but gain, gratitude, and overwhelming joy will be the dominant emotion. Randy Alcorn notes:

> Still, the primary purpose of the bema is not loss, but gain. Even though the consequences of missed opportunities and lost reward will go with us into eternity, any regret or shame we might experience will not. How can I be sure? Because the Bible promises that "God will wipe away every tear from their eyes" (Revelation 21:4). The amazing truth is that, regardless of what happens at the bema, Jesus will not love you any less or any more for eternity than He loved you when He purchased your life with His own blood—or than He loves you right now.[11]

Joe Wall observes:

> The negative part of the bema judgment may be similar to the time when Peter stood near Christ during His trial. Jesus looked over at the man who had denied

Him three times and He convicted him with the eyes of betrayed love—not with vindictive words, but with the gentle reproach of someone who truly understood Peter's human fears. His will not be an antagonistic legal judgment by someone who desires to punish us. It will be the loving judgment of the One who died for us.[12]

Whatever loss or remorse we may feel at the judgment seat will quickly go away. No one will live forever in heaven feeling like a second-class citizen. Our appearance at the *bema* will be joyful above all else. "Now to Him who is able to keep you from stumbling, and to make you stand in the presence of His glory blameless with great joy, to the only God our Savior, through Jesus Christ our Lord, be glory, majesty, dominion and authority, before all time and now and forever. Amen" (Jude 24-25). Any remorse we experience will eventually be washed over by a wave of inexpressible joy. We will stand in our Lord's presence with great joy.

Employing a helpful illustration, Samuel Hoyt strikes an excellent balance between the remorse and rejoicing believers will experience at the *bema* judgment:

> The judgment seat of Christ might be compared to a commencement ceremony. At graduation there is some measure of disappointment and remorse that one did not do better and work harder. However, at such an event the overwhelming emotion is joy, not remorse. The graduates do not leave the auditorium weeping because they did not earn better grades. Rather, they are thankful that they have been graduated, and they are grateful for what they did achieve. To overdo the sorrow aspect of the judgment seat of Christ is to make heaven hell. To underdo the sorrow aspect is to make faithfulness inconsequential.[13]

The day you and I stand before the Lord will be the most conse-
quential moment of our lives. Nothing will ever come close to it. Live
today to do all you can to reduce your regret and boost your bliss.

Will our evaluation by Jesus at the judgment seat be public or private?

When I was a boy and heard sermons about the day of judgment
before the Lord, I always imagined that all my sins, sordid thoughts,
and weakest moments would be projected on a huge video screen
(this was back in the day before big-screen TVs and HD). I pictured myself cringing in embarrassment and shame as the evaluation seems like it lasts for eternity. All my deepest secrets and dirtiest
laundry would be exposed to my parents, my pastor, my friends,
and a host of believers I had never met. Of course, my childish perspective was misguided. Our sins won't be under review at the judgment seat. They were paid for by the death of Jesus. Yet the question
remains—will each of us be reviewed privately, or will the review
be public?

Some emphasize the individual nature of the judgment seat by
pointing to passages such as Romans 14:12, which seems to indicate
the review will be private. Woodrow Kroll holds this view: "Besides,
a private evaluation of our life and work is only natural. It is really
nobody else's business what we have done for the Lord or why we
have done it. This is a matter that concerns just you and your Judge
(see John 2:20-23)."[14]

While this is certainly possible, I believe the Lord's evaluation
will take place in the presence of others, including angels. After all,
Jesus promised to confess His followers before them (Luke 12:8).
Remember how, in the parable of the minas, the unfaithful slave
who hid his mina was castigated? Note what the king did: "Then
he said to the bystanders, 'Take the mina away from him and give
it to the one who has the ten minas'" (Luke 19:24). When it comes
to parables we must be careful to not press every detail for meaning,

but note here that the judgment was public. Others were present to observe what happened and even participated.

The public nature of our final accounting may be unsettling to you, but remember: We will all be in the same boat. None of us will have anything to gloat about. We will all have plenty of bad to go along with anything good. As Erwin Lutzer says,

> I'm convinced that when we look into the eyes of Christ, what others think will not matter. A student giving a recital on the piano cares only what his teacher thinks. To a football player, the censure or affirmation of the coach means much more than the boos or cheers of the fans. In the presence of Christ, we will be oblivious to those around us. The expression on His face will tell it all.[15]

What are the rewards for "overcomers" mentioned in the book of Revelation?

At the end of each of the seven letters to the churches in Revelation 2–3, Jesus promised special rewards to "overcomers." The seven promised rewards are...

1. Special access to the tree of life (2:7).

2. Protection from the second death (2:10-11).

3. Provision of hidden manna and a white stone with a name known only to the recipient (2:17).

4. The morning star (2:28).

5. Being clothed in white garments and confessed before the Father and the angels (3:5).

6. Becoming a pillar in the temple of God and having the name of God and the heavenly city written upon us (3:12).

7. Sitting with Christ on His throne in the messianic kingdom (3:21).

The apostle John uses the word "overcome" in its various form seven times in 1 John and seventeen times in Revelation. The Greek word is *nikao* (the athletic apparel company Nike gets its name from this word, which is the name of the Greek goddess of victory).

Some people have asked whether overcomers refers to all believers, or only to a special class of Christians who are especially faithful to the Lord and have exceled in their victory over the world. There are two key reasons to believe that John was including every believer in his use of overcomer.

First, several of the promises to the overcomers in Revelation 2–3 are clearly offered to every Christian and not just some. Here are three examples:

1. Revelation 2:7 says, "To him who overcomes, I will grant to eat of the tree of life which is in the Paradise of God." Every believer will have access to the tree of life, not only some special group of the faithful.

2. In Revelation 2:11, the overcomers in Smyrna are promised, "He who overcomes will not be hurt by the second death." The second death is hell (20:14), and this promise is true of every believer. It's not limited to those who have attained some special status.[16]

3. In the letter to the church at Sardis, Jesus said, "He who overcomes will thus be clothed in white garments; and I will not erase his name from the book of life, and I will confess his name before My Father and before His angels." The negation in the original Greek text is emphatic. Jesus literally said, "I will never ever erase the name of an overcomer from the book of life." This is a strong word of assurance to all who trust in Christ. As overcomers by faith,

our name can never be erased from God's book.[17] Also, the promise of having your name confessed before the Father and His angels is true of every believer, not a select few (Matthew 10:32-33).

A second convincing reason to understand the overcomers in Revelation 2–3 as all believers is 1 John 5:4-5, which says, "Whatever is born of God overcomes the world; and this is the victory that has overcome the world—our faith. Who is the one who overcomes the world, but he who believes that Jesus is the Son of God?" John, the human author of both 1 John and Revelation, defines an overcomer as a believer in Jesus Christ.[18] It would be strange for John to change his meaning of an overcomer without giving clear indication that he's doing so.

Referring to the overcomers in Revelation 2–3, John MacArthur says, "The term does not refer to those who have attained to a higher level of the Christian life, but identifies all Christians. The apostle John defines it that way in his first epistle...All true believers are overcomers, who have by God's grace and power overcome the damning power of the evil world system."[19]

Will our lives from *before* we came to Christ be part of our review?

How much of our lives will be under review at the judgment seat? Will our entire life be subject to examination, or only the portion after we became believers? Scripture is clear that we will only be judged for what we've done and how we've lived after our conversion to Christ. The apostle Paul anticipated a favorable outcome at the judgment seat, yet he had imprisoned, persecuted, and even murdered believers before his conversion to Christ.

I am already being poured out as a drink offering, and the time of my departure has come. I have fought the good fight, I have finished the course, I have kept the faith; in the future there is laid up for me the crown of righteousness, which the Lord, the righteous Judge, will award to me on that day; and not only to me, but also to all who have loved His appearing (2 Timothy 4:6-8).

Knowing that our pre-conversion life won't be subject to review at the judgment seat should be a great comfort and relief to us all, especially those who lived terribly sinful and debauched lives before coming to Christ. Part of the good news at the judgment seat is that "we'll not be judged on what we did from the time of our *first* birth, but on what we did since our *second* birth."[20] Rewards will be dispensed based on our faithfulness to the opportunities we've had since our conversion.

There's Always Another Question

There are still more questions people have—for example, What rewards will we receive in heaven? How will we be rewarded? What will make our heavenly rewards different from earthly ones?

We'll learn more answers in the next chapter.

CHAPTER SIX

Gaining What You Can't Lose

*He is no fool who gives what he cannot
keep, to gain what he cannot lose.*

Jim Eliot

Rewards are a part of life. From our earliest years we get gold stars on our homework from our teachers for a job well done, blue ribbons at the county fair, and trophies for participating in sports. As we grow older the rewards get more expensive and more difficult to earn, and if we're honest, we all have appreciated being recognized and rewarded for a job well done. Most rewards are simple and basic, but there are some that have become so prestigious that they are widely coveted and celebrated all over the world.

- The green jacket for winning The Masters golf tournament
- The yellow jersey at the Tour de France
- The Pulitzer Prize
- A Super Bowl ring
- An Olympic medal

- The Nobel Peace Prize
- An Oscar
- An Emmy
- The Purple Heart
- The Congressional Medal of Honor

As satisfying as it must be to receive one of these earthly honors, they pale in comparison to the smile we will receive from our Savior as He bestows His rewards on us. The ultimate rewards are given by God. Few would dispute that divine rewards are the zenith of recognition. So what rewards will God give to His children in heaven? What should we expect? Are rewards merely a good feeling? Are they tangible? Are they crowns? If so, what is a crown?

The Nature of Heavenly Rewards

Although the full nature of eternal rewards is something we will never fully understand here on Earth, we can discern a few basic elements of these rewards based on what we read in Scripture.

Praise—Commendation

The first heavenly reward we will receive from the Lord is His praise. Here are a few verses that speak of our future commendation.

"Do not go on passing judgment before the time, but wait until the Lord comes who will both bring to light the things hidden in the darkness and disclose the motives of men's hearts; and then each man's praise will come to him from God" (1 Corinthians 4:5).

In His parable of the talents, the Master said to his first two servants, "Well done, good and faithful slave. You were faithful with a few things, I will put you in charge of many things; enter into the joy of your master" (Matthew 25:21, 23).

We all know how great it is to be praised by a parent, spouse, or boss for a job well done. Think of what it will be like to stand before the Lord and hear Him say, "Well done." The Creator of heaven and Earth—our Maker—will praise you and me for good works done with acceptable motives. Nothing will match that moment. No reward in this life can ever compare to the praise we will receive from the Master in heaven. "His commendation will be worth whatever it costs to merit it."[1]

Position—Co-Ruling

A second reward will be reigning or co-ruling with Christ. Faithful service for Christ here on Earth will bring positions of rule and authority in the coming kingdom and on into the eternal state. Ruling with and for Christ will be the culmination of God's original creation. The creation account in Genesis 1–2 reveals that God created Adam and Eve in His image and placed them in paradise (the Garden of Eden) to enjoy intimate fellowship with their Creator and to rule on His behalf.

> God said, "Let Us make man in Our image, according to Our likeness; and let them rule over the fish of the sea and over the birds of the sky and over the cattle and over all the earth, and over every creeping thing that creeps on the earth." God created man in His own image, in the image of God He created him; male and female He created them. God blessed them; and God said to them, "Be fruitful and multiply, and fill the earth, and subdue it; and rule over the fish of the sea and over the birds of the sky and over every living thing that moves on the earth" (Genesis 1:26-28).

Adam and Eve were created to serve as co-rulers with the Triune God over the newly created planet. Tragically, human rulership over Earth was forfeited through open treason against the Creator when the man and woman ate of the forbidden fruit. Satan, the great antagonist and usurper, then assumed authority over Earth. He became the ruler (John 12:31) and god of this world (2 Corinthians 4:4).

God's solution to this crisis was to promise a redeemer who would crush the head of the serpent (Genesis 3:15). The rest of the Bible, from that point onward, looks to the coming of this promised one. The Old Testament is filled with prophecies and promises of His coming, and the Gospels tell us about the arrival of the promised One, Jesus Christ, and His death and resurrection to atone for sin and redeem fallen people and creation.

Today, we live in the interim between the climax of the story and its consummation at the second advent of Christ. We're awaiting the return of the Lord, the last Adam, who is coming to take the inheritance of the nations and do what the first Adam failed to do (Psalm 2:8; Revelation 11:15). The Bible is clear—a man will rule over the earth as God intended from the beginning. God is determined to fulfill His purpose for this world and mankind. What was lost will be gloriously regained when Jesus comes to defeat Satan and his final imposter, the Antichrist, at Armageddon (Revelation 19:11-21).

When Jesus takes the inheritance and establishes His reign over the earth for 1,000 years (phase 1 of the kingdom), then continues to rule forever in the eternal kingdom (phase 2), we will reign with Him.

- "If we endure, we will also reign with Him" (2 Timothy 2:12).

- "He who overcomes, I will grant to him to sit down with Me on My throne, as I also overcame and sat down with My Father on His throne" (Revelation 3:21).

- "You have made them to be a kingdom and priests to our God; and they will reign upon the earth" (Revelation 5:10).

- "There will no longer be any night; and they will not have need of the light of a lamp nor the light of the sun, because

the Lord God will illumine them; and they will reign forever and ever" (Revelation 22:5).

The positions of authority we are given in the future are being
determined now by how we live. Our stewardship of our time,
opportunities, and resources will determine the degree of our
authority. Jesus said that some will rule over ten cities, and others
will rule over five (Luke 19:17-19). Our lives today are training time
for reigning time.

In his excellent book *Heaven*, Randy Alcorn says,

> Notice that the Master rewards his faithful servants not
> by taking away responsibilities but by giving them greater
> ones.
>
> Service is a reward, not a punishment. This idea is
> foreign to people who dislike their work and only put
> up with it until retirement. We think that faithful work
> should be rewarded by a vacation for the rest of our lives.
> But God offers us something very different: more work,
> more responsibilities, increased opportunities, along with
> greater abilities, resources, wisdom, and empowerment.
> We will have sharp minds, strong bodies, clear purpose,
> and unabated joy. The more we serve Christ now, the
> greater our capacity will be to serve him in Heaven.
>
> Reigning over cities will certainly not be "having
> nothing to do." I believe that those who rule on the New
> Earth will have leisure (rest) and will fully enjoy it, but
> they will also have plenty to do.[2]

He continues:

> Should we be excited that God will reward us by making
> us ruler in his Kingdom? Absolutely. Jesus said, "Rejoice

and be glad, because great is your reward in heaven"
(Matthew 5:12).

God will choose who reigns as kings, and I think
some great surprises are in store for us. Christ gives us
clues in Scripture as to the type of person he will choose:
"Blessed are the poor in spirit, for theirs is the kingdom
of heaven...Blessed are the meek, for they will inherit
the earth. Blessed are those who are persecuted because
of righteousness, for theirs is the kingdom of heaven"
(Matthew 5:3, 5, 10). "'God opposes the proud but
gives grace to the humble.' Humble yourselves, therefore, under God's mighty hand, that he may lift you up
in due time" (1 Peter 5:5-6).

Look around you to see the meek and the humble.[3]

We see them all around us every day. They may include bus driv-
ers, construction workers, lawyers, accountants, mechanics, and stay-
at-home moms who spend their days tirelessly carpooling, changing
diapers, cooking dinner, packing lunches, and drying tears.

Randy Alcorn shares this moving story to illustrate this point.

> I once gave one of my books to a delightful hotel bell-
> man. I discovered he was a committed Christian. He
> said he'd been praying for our group, which was holding
> a conference at the hotel. Later, I gave him a little gift, a
> rough wooden cross. He seemed stunned, overwhelmed.
> With tears in his eyes he said, "You didn't need to do that.
> I'm only a bellman." The moment he said it, I realized
> that this brother had spent his life serving. It will likely
> be someone like him that I'll have the privilege of serv-
> ing under in God's Kingdom. He was "only a bellman,"
> who spoke with such warmth and love, who served, who
> quietly prayed in the background for the success of a

conference in his hotel. I saw Jesus in that bellman, and there was no "only" about him.

Who will be the kings of the New Earth? I think that bellman will be one of them. And I'll be honored to carry his bags.[4]

Another part of our ruling with and for Christ will be to judge angels, according to 1 Corinthians 6:2-3. Our judging the angels won't involve bringing them to justice, because they will not sin. Rather, it will entail exercising authority and rule over them. This may be part of what makes Satan so angry. "The fact that sinful human beings, who sided with him in Eden, will be exalted above the angelic realm of which he was at one time a member is more than he can bear."[5]

Much about our reward of co-ruling with Christ remains a mystery, but the application to our lives today is clear. We remain faithful and endure hardship now because we know there's a throne awaiting us in the future.

Privilege—Crowns

The third kind of reward the Lord will give at the judgment seat is privileges and honors. These privileges come in two forms, with the first being crowns.

A bit of background here is helpful. As we've already seen, the city of Corinth, in Greece, was the apostle Paul's headquarters during his second missionary journey. He spent eighteen months there preaching and teaching God's Word (Acts 18:11). Not far from Corinth were the Isthmian Games. As New Testament scholar Gordon Fee notes,

> These games, held every two years under the patronage of Corinth and second only to the Olympics, were extravagant festivals of religion, athletics, and the arts,

attracting thousands of competitors and visitors from all over the empire...Paul would have been in Corinth during the games of A.D. 51 (in the spring).[6]

Crowns were awarded at these games. Now, when we hear of a crown, usually we think of beautiful, glistening, golden royal crowns with jewels. But the crowns given to the victors at the ancient games were not the *diadema* or royal crown, but the *stephanos* crown. which was like a wreath or garland made from twisted leaves, pine shoots, parsley, or olive branches. In spite of its humble appearance, the *stephanos* was the gold medal of its day and brought great honor and benefits to the victor—in the same way that a gold medal does for today's Olympic athletes.

The New Testament outlines five different crowns that the Lord will bestow on the faithful at the *bema* judgment.

1. The Incorruptible / Imperishable Crown

Also known as the crown of mastery or discipline, this reward is for those who consistently practice self-control and master the temptations of the sins of the flesh.

> Do you not know that those who run in a race all run, but only one receives the prize? Run in such a way that you may win. Everyone who competes in the games exercises self-control in all things. They then do it to receive a perishable wreath, but we an imperishable. Therefore I run in such a way, as not without aim; I box in such a way, as not beating the air; but I discipline my body and make it my slave, so that, after I have preached to others, I myself will not be disqualified (1 Corinthians 9:24-27).

The Lord greatly values self-discipline and self-control over the temptations related to our physical bodies.

2. The Crown of Righteousness

At the moment of salvation, every believer receives the righteousness of Jesus Christ. Without His righteousness, we cannot be saved and enter heaven. The crown of righteousness is a special capacity to enjoy righteousness given to those who eagerly look for the Lord's coming and live a righteous life in view of this fact. This crown is sometimes called "the watcher's crown." This reward "refers to the crown awarded for finishing the race of life righteously, with our eyes on Jesus, especially anticipating His return."

The apostle Paul spoke of this crown in the waning days of his life on Earth and looked forward to securing it for himself. He said, "I have fought the good fight, I have finished the course, I have kept the faith; in the future there is laid up for me the crown of righteousness, which the Lord, the righteous Judge, will award to me on that day; and not only to me, but also to all who have loved His appearing" (1 Timothy 4:7-8).

Looking eagerly for the coming of Christ is a powerful incentive to godly living. An awareness of the Lord's coming exerts a cleansing, purifying effect on our lives. "Beloved, now we are children of God, and it has not appeared as yet what we will be. We know that when He appears, we will be like Him, because we will see Him just as He is. And everyone who has this hope fixed on Him purifies himself, just as He is pure" (1 John 3:2-3). "Holy living is the sure sign of heavenly longing."[7]

Are you yearning for Christ's coming, or yawning? Do you long for His appearing? Are you ready for the rapture? Is the anticipation of His coming motivating you to live a righteous life?

3. The Crown of Life

Every Christian receives eternal life. The crown of life is the sufferer's or martyr's crown given to those who faithfully endure, persevere, and hang in there under the trials and tests of life, including the greatest test, which is martyrdom. The recipients of this crown will enjoy life to its fullest. This crown is mentioned in two New Testament passages:

- "Blessed is a man who perseveres under trial; for once he has been approved, he will receive the crown of life which the Lord has promised to those who love Him" (James 1:12).

- "Do not fear what you are about to suffer. Behold, the devil is about to cast some of you into prison, so that you will be tested, and you will have tribulation for ten days. Be faithful until death, and I will give you the crown of life" (Revelation 2:10).

Every Christian can receive this reward because we all face suffering, trials, and troubles in life. May the Lord strengthen us all to remain steadfast in the face of affliction and receive the crown of life.

4. The Crown of Rejoicing

The soul-winner's crown will be given to those who win people for Christ. "Who is our hope or joy or crown of exultation? Is it not even you, in the presence of our Lord Jesus at His coming?" (1 Thessalonians 2:19). "Therefore, my beloved brethren whom I long to see, my joy and crown, in this way stand firm in the Lord, my beloved" (Philippians 4:1). This crown symbolizes people to whom we've ministered and pointed to Christ.

>...when we stand in the presence of Jesus at His royal coming, our hearts will overflow with pride, joy, and exultation because of those who stand with us at that time—those we have had a share in bringing to the Savior.
>
>What a thrill! For all eternity we will have "walking wreath-crowns" living and enjoying with us the glorious presence and unspeakable delights of life in the kingdom of the Prince of Peace.[8]

Not every believer has the gift of evangelism, but we're all called to be witnesses to the saving grace of Jesus Christ. How long has it been since you shared the good news of the gospel with a friend or coworker?

There's no thrill in life like that of leading another person to Christ. This crown is aptly named "the crown of rejoicing" because heaven will be filled with rejoicing when we stand before the Lord with those who have come to Christ through our witness.

5. *The Crown of Glory*

The shepherd's crown will be given to those pastors, elders, and church leaders who lovingly, graciously, and faithfully feed, lead, guide, and oversee God's people.

> I exhort the elders among you, as your fellow elder and witness of the sufferings of Christ, and a partaker also of the glory that is to be revealed, shepherd the flock of God among you, exercising oversight not under compulsion, but voluntarily, according to the will of God; and not for sordid gain, but with eagerness; nor yet as lording it over those allotted to your charge, but proving to be examples to the flock. And when the Chief Shepherd appears, you will receive the unfading crown of glory (1 Peter 5:1-4).

Having served for nearly thirty years as a pastor of a local church with many elders and a pastoral staff in all kinds of difficult situations, I can understand why the Lord would tailor a special reward for faithful church leaders. Decisions can be difficult. Criticism, often harsh and unwarranted, must be patiently endured. Countless hours are expended in planning, budgeting, prayer, Bible study, sermon preparation, visiting the sick and bereaved, conducting weddings and funerals. I've been blessed to serve shoulder to shoulder with dozens of faithful men who love the Lord's flock and are gracious and loving. I trust that many of them will receive this crown.

Every Christian is eligible to receive the rewards mentioned above, except the crown of glory, which is reserved for pastors and elders. I believe it's possible for believers to win more than one crown. We should labor faithfully and sacrificially now to secure these heavenly rewards.

We are told in Revelation 4:10-11 what will happen after we receive these rewards:

> The twenty-four elders will fall down before Him who sits on the throne, and will worship Him who lives forever and ever, and will cast their crowns before the throne, saying, "Worthy are You, our Lord and our God, to receive glory and honor and power; for You created all things, and because of Your will they existed, and were created."

Casting our crowns at the feet of the One who sits on the throne will be an act of supreme worship as well as an acknowledgement that everything we are and have accomplished is ultimately due to His grace and goodness. This will be our way of giving Him unreserved glory and praise.

The casting of crowns before the Lord does not mean that rewards will be surrendered to Christ and will play no future part in our lives in heaven. After this event, believers will return with Christ to the earth and enjoy different positions of rule and authority during His millennial reign (Matthew 25:31-46). The rewards we gain will carry on for all eternity.

Erwin Lutzer believes the Lord may give the crowns back to us. He says,

If we are given actual crowns in heaven, I'm sure we
will gladly lay them at Christ's feet. But it is wrong to
think that our rewards are crowns and nothing more...I
believe He shall give them back to us so we can join Him
in ruling "forever and ever"...Whatever might happen to
the crowns, our rewards are eternal.[9]

Think of what it will be like to receive a crown from the nail-
pierced hands of Jesus. He will give the reward personally. "Awards
aren't given a nation at a time, a church at a time, or a generation at
a time. The crowns are given one at a time."[10] Then we will have the
privilege of casting them at the feet of Him who sits on the throne.

Some might wonder: Are rewards really that big of a deal? Randy
Alcorn underscores the shortsightedness of many believers when he
says,

Most Christians have heard about eternal rewards, but
many consider them to be figurative—nice words about
crowns, but come on, who wants a crown anyway. A
chalet in the mountains, a new boat, golfing on the
finest courses and going to the Bahamas...doesn't that
sound like a lot more fun? Why wait for something later
that doesn't sound so great anyway?[11]

Make no mistake. Our heavenly rewards will be great. Whatever we must sacrifice here to receive those rewards will be well
worthwhile.

Another way to look at our rewards as honors or privileges is that
they will reflect the amount of God's glory that shines through us.
Daniel 12:2-3 says,

Many of those who sleep in the dust of the ground will
awake, these to everlasting life, but the others to disgrace

and everlasting contempt. Those who have insight will shine brightly like the brightness of the expanse of heaven, and those who lead the many to righteousness, like the stars forever and ever.

Jesus quoted Daniel 12:3 in Matthew 13:43 when He said, "The righteous will shine forth as the sun in the kingdom of their Father. He who has ears, let him hear."

All of God's people together in eternity will be like a dazzling chandelier with many lightbulbs—some twenty-five watts, some fifty watts, and some one hundred watts or more. The lightbulbs, as a whole, will shine light in the room. They will all contribute, with some shining brighter than others. That's the way it will be in heaven. Some of us will contribute twenty-five watts, others fifty, and still others one hundred or even more. We will be vessels of God's glory. No one will feel slighted or insignificant. We will all shine. The question is, "How much of God's light do you want to shine through you?" The venerable Bible teacher and professor J. Dwight Pentecost said,

> Inasmuch as reward is associated with brightness and shining in many passages of Scripture (Dan. 12:3; Matt. 13:43; 1 Cor. 15:40-41, 49), it may be that the reward given to the believer is a capacity to manifest the glory of Christ throughout eternity. The greater the reward, the greater the bestowed capacity to bring glory to God...Capacities to radiate the glory will differ, but there will be no personal sense of lack in that each believer will be filled to the limit of his capacity.[12]

No one will experience a lack of fullness or feel incomplete. One way to express this thought is that everyone's cup in heaven will be full, but some cups will be larger than others. Some will possess a greater capacity and capability to glorify the Lord.

Payday Is Coming

Even after we consider what the Bible says about the rewards we will receive, there are still many unanswered questions. In His wisdom, God has communicated enough information to us so that we can know some general facts about the rewards that await us. What we can say without hesitation is that at this present time, our future rewards are far beyond our ability to comprehend and appreciate. As Max Lucado says, "While we're not sure exactly what those rewards are, we do know they include heavenly applause, God's approval, and eternal life. What else would you want?"[13]

There's an old poem titled "Who Does God's Work Will Get God's Pay." Meditate on these words and let them motivate you to sacrifice for the Lord in light of the coming day when you will stand before Him.

Who does God's work will get God's pay,
However long may be the day.
He does not pay as others pay,
In gold, or land, or raiment gay,
In goods that perish or decay;
But God's high wisdom knows the way,
And this is sure, let come what may—
Who does God's work will get God's pay.

Writer unknown

CHAPTER SEVEN

Use It or Lose It

*If you don't want to use the army, I
should like to borrow it for a while.*[1]

Yours respectfully, A. Lincoln

I have a recurring dream, or what I would call a nightmare, which I've read is common among those who have been to college or spent a lot of time in school. In this dream, which seems so real, it's the end of the semester, and I suddenly realize that I haven't been attending a class that I had registered for. The final exam is looming ahead of me, and I'm *totally panicked* because I haven't done the work for the class. I can't figure out what's going on. I'm scurrying around trying to get ready, trying to make up for lost time, but it's too late.

Have you ever had that dream? It's crazy, isn't it?

Thankfully, at some point I wake up and realize that I'm off the hook. It was only a dream. I feel an incredible sense of relief.

But what if it were true? Have you ever thought about that? And what if it was not just a college class, but the end of the age and the examiner was the Lord? You realize too late that you must give an account to Him, and you've not been doing what you were supposed to have done. You're totally unprepared. You've been lazy and indifferent. And it's too late to get ready. That would be an awful nightmare from which you wouldn't wake up!

The parable Jesus told His followers in Luke 19:11-27 is a wake-up call that every person will face a day of reckoning—a final test—when all their actions and inactions will be weighed. It's often called the Parable of the Pounds, or the Parable of the Minas.

The main point of this parable is simple yet striking: *Because we will all be called to account someday when Jesus returns, we must trust the Master and faithfully invest what He's given us to maximize the return.*

> While they were listening to these things, Jesus went on to tell a parable, because He was near Jerusalem, and they supposed that the kingdom of God was going to appear immediately. So He said, "A nobleman went to a distant country to receive a kingdom for himself, and then return. And he called ten of his slaves, and gave them ten minas and said to them, 'Do business with this until I come back.' But his citizens hated him and sent a delegation after him, saying, 'We do not want this man to reign over us.' When he returned, after receiving the kingdom, he ordered that these slaves, to whom he had given the money, be called to him so that he might know what business they had done. The first appeared, saying, 'Master, your mina has made ten minas more.' And he said to him, 'Well done, good slave, because you have been faithful in a very little thing, you are to be in authority over ten cities.' The second came, saying, 'Your mina, master, has made five minas.' And he said to him also, 'And you are to be over five cities.' Another came, saying, 'Master, here is your mina, which I kept put away in a handkerchief; for I was afraid of you, because

you are an exacting man; you take up what you did not lay down and reap what you did not sow.' He said to him, 'By your own words I will judge you, you worthless slave. Did you know that I am an exacting man, taking up what I did not lay down and reaping what I did not sow? Then why did you not put my money in the bank, and having come, I would have collected it with interest?' Then he said to the bystanders, 'Take the mina away from him and give it to the one who has the ten minas.' And they said to him, 'Master, he has ten minas already.' I tell you that to everyone who has, more shall be given, but from the one who does not have, even what he does have shall be taken away. But these enemies of mine, who did not want me to reign over them, bring them here and slay them in my presence."

The Prince of Parables

Other than end-time prophecies, my favorite Bible study topic is the parables of Jesus. The stories Jesus told are fascinating and always contain a twist or surprise that packs a spiritual punch. There's something about the parables that pulls us into the story and jolts us to align our thinking and living with its truth. Warren Wiersbe said, "The parables are both mirrors and windows. As mirrors they help us see ourselves. They reveal our lives as they really are. As windows, they help us see life and God."[2]

One-third of Jesus's speaking ministry was in the form of parables. The root meaning of the word *parable* (*parabole* in Greek) suggests putting things side by side, and broadly speaking, a parable is just that—a putting together of ideas from different spheres in such a way that one idea illuminates another. In a parable, there is a transference from the known to the unknown. A simple definition of a parable is "an earthly story with a heavenly meaning."

The Focus of the Parables

While Jesus's parables deal with an assortment of topics, the central focus of them is the coming of the kingdom of God and the resulting discipleship that is required. This parable is no exception.

To unpack this parable, we'll gather our thoughts around three simple points:

1. The Setting
2. The Story
3. The Significance

Every one of us will find ourselves in this parable.

The Setting

The time is late March, AD 33, just days before Jesus's final week on Earth. Jesus is in Jericho, the city of the palms, on the final leg of His journey to Jerusalem that began in Luke 9:51. Jericho is about seventeen miles from Jerusalem. The road from Jericho to Jerusalem takes about six hours to navigate because it's a steep uphill grade. Jesus and His followers were traveling to Jerusalem for the last time for Passover.

The closer the entourage got to Jerusalem, the greater the enthusiasm became around them. Soon Jesus would enter Jerusalem to the triumphant cheers proclaiming Him as King (Luke 19:28-38). Kingdom anticipation was building, and excitement was running high. Verse 11 tells us that as Jesus arrived in Jericho, "they supposed that the kingdom of God was going to appear immediately." The people thought they had finally found the promised deliverer who would throw off the Roman government's yoke of bondage. They believed the kingdom would appear and Jesus would establish His messianic reign on Earth, as promised repeatedly in the Old Testament.

Jesus spoke the Parable of the Pounds to allay people's incorrect expectations about the arrival of the kingdom. Instead, He wanted them to know how they should live during the interim between His going away and coming again. Jesus's followers didn't realize that He would suffer and die, be raised from the dead, ascend into heaven, and that many years (now two millennia) would pass before He returned to establish His kingdom on Earth.

The Story

Jesus, the master teacher, based this story about the coming of the kingdom on a historical incident that had taken place about thirty years earlier—an event that happened the year Jesus was born (4 BC).

Here's what happened: King Herod, known as Herod the Great, died in 4 BC. His kingdom was divided among his three sons, with Archelaus receiving half of the kingdom (Judea, Samaria, and Idumea). Some people came to Archelaus in the city of Jericho and wanted to make him king. Archelaus knew that only Caesar Augustus in Rome could confer that title, so he traveled to Rome with a large entourage, seeking the title. To his surprise, some of his own family members opposed this. Also, a contingent of fifty Jews followed Archelaus from Israel to Rome to protest his installation as king and to lodge a formal complaint with Caesar. In Rome, another 8,000 Jews joined the opposition, accusing Archelaus of ineptness and corruption.

Augustus, realizing he had a problem on his hands, ordered a compromise. He gave Archelaus the title—*ethnarch*—and told him he had to earn the title, which he never did.

Armed with his new title, Archelaus returned to Israel and rewarded those who were faithful to him in his absence and punished those who were not.

Jesus used this familiar storyline of an event that began in Jericho as the backdrop for this parable. He pictured Himself as a nobleman going away to receive a kingdom, and His followers as His servants whom He had left behind to do business with His resources while they awaited His return.

Some people believe this parable in Luke 19 is another version of the Parable of the Talents in Matthew 25. While there are some similarities, there are significant differences that indicate the two parables are different stories:

	Matthew 25:14-30	**Luke 19:11-27**
Place	In Jerusalem	Approaching Jerusalem
Time	Two days before His death	At least one week before His death
Main Character	A man	A nobleman who becomes king
Money	Talent (75 pounds of silver)	Mina (3 months' wages)
Number of Slaves	Three	Ten
Amount	Each given different amount	Each given same amount
People	Only slaves	Slaves and citizens

The story Jesus told in Luke 19 unfolds in two parts.

The Nobleman Departs—Assignment of the Servants

The story opened with the departure of a nobleman to a distant country to receive a kingdom. Before he left, he called upon ten of his slaves. Each was given a mina, which was about one hundred days' wages, equal to about $20,000 in our day. Each servant was given the same amount. The mina represents the responsibilities, opportunities, and resources our Lord gives to His servants to invest for Him. Every believer has a mina.

The nobleman's instructions were simple and clear: "Do business with this until I come back" (Luke 19:13). The King James Version translates this, "Occupy till I come." The Living Bible paraphrases this, saying the slaves were to "invest while he was gone." Jesus wanted His hearers to know what they were supposed to be doing in His absence. They were not supposed to sit around waiting for Him to return. Rather, they were to be actively doing business for Him with what He had entrusted to them.

The mandate is to maximize our opportunities.

The Nobleman Returns—Accounting of the Servants

In scene two of the story, the nobleman returned from his long absence, and the plot thickened. Unlike Archelaus, who was a wannabe king, Jesus is the true King. Jesus wanted His first-century followers to know that His kingdom would not come immediately. There would be a delay. He would be gone for a while. Jesus said there would be an extended interim between His comings, but the kingdom *will* come. Nothing can stop it. When Christ comes back, He will do so as King, and when He returns, there will be an accounting—a day of reckoning. Each servant will be required to give an account for what he has done. There will be no place to hide, no excuses. Whatever you did or didn't do with your mina will be fully manifest.

In the final reckoning, for the sake of brevity, only three of the ten servants are mentioned, but the three are clearly representative of the rest. The first two servants Jesus spoke to were faithful. Let's look at what He said to them.

First Servant (Report and Reward)

When the first slave was called to give his account, he said, "Master, your mina has made ten minas more" (verse 16). Notice he didn't say, "Look what I did." He was humble. He recognized that it all belonged to God. He called the mina "*your* mina." This is a key to successful service—remembering that your opportunities and resources come from God. We must say to God, "Your mina did it—all I did was put it to work."

The slave reported an astounding profit of 1,000 percent. He took $20,000 and turned it into $200,000. The reward for this return was astoundingly generous. Look at what he received—ten entire cities to rule over in the future kingdom. Think of the great cities of our world: Sydney, Honolulu, Rome, Barcelona, or beautiful places like the Greek isles. In the coming kingdom, when Jesus reigns over the earth for 1,000 years, God's people will rule with Him (see Revelation 5:11). And this rule will continue on into the eternal kingdom (Revelation 22:5).

There's an important lesson here that we must not miss: *The rewards for investing are huge.* R. Kent Hughes noted the extravagance of the future rewards: "The reward of Christ's faithful servants is an elevation of eternal intimacy with Him. They will be co-regents, viceroys, and confidants. What joy! Happily, the eternal reward is not rest but responsibility as we work with Christ in unimaginably vast new spiritual enterprises."[3]

The compensation we will receive for faithfulness is colossal.

The Second Servant (Report and Reward)

Slave two came forward to give an accounting and announced that he took his $20,000 and turned it into $100,000 (a 500 percent profit). In return, he was given five cities to rule over. This teaches us that faithfulness even in small things can bring great reward. As the renowned missionary Hudson Taylor said, "A little thing is a little thing, but faithfulness in a little thing is a great thing."

There's an old maxim that says, "If it sounds too good to be true, it probably is." Yet here it really is true: God is lavish and generous with His rewards.

The greater the faithfulness in this life, the greater the reward and responsibility in the next. The present is our training ground for the future, our *training time for reigning time.*

The Third Servant (Report and Rebuke)

We come now to the final servant. When Jesus spoke in parables, He often employed a rhetorical technique known as "end stress," which means that the end of the parable contained a surprising twist and stress that informs the meaning of the story. The focus in this parable is on the third servant—much more is said about him than the first two, who were faithful. This third servant was clearly different. Rather than investing the master's mina, he simply stashed it away, hiding it in a handkerchief.

An important question arises about this unfaithful servant that must be answered: Does he represent an unfruitful, carnal believer who doesn't live for the Lord and loses his rewards? Or is he a person who professes to know Christ but has no relationship with Him? There are good Bible teachers and commentators on both sides of this debate.

Those who believe the third slave is a true believer who loses his rewards point to the fact that he received a mina just like the first two servants. Also, they note that he isn't included with the enemies of the nobleman in verse 27.

Notwithstanding those two arguments, four key points lead me to believe this servant represents someone who professes to know Christ but has no relationship with Him—a false follower.

First, in verse 20, the third servant was introduced by the words "And another came." The first two servants were introduced with the words "the first appeared" (verse 16) and "the second appeared" (verse 18). When Jesus spoke about the third servant, He didn't maintain the same formula and say "the third appeared." Instead, he said, "And another came." The Greek word translated "another" is the word *heteros*, which means "another of a different kind." In using this word, Jesus was tipping us off that this slave is not like the first two. He's of another kind.

Second, Jesus called him "you worthless slave" (verse 22). The Greek word used here is often translated "evil" or "wicked." This seems like a rather strange way for Jesus to describe one of His followers.

Third, while the parable of the talents in Matthew 25:14-30 is not identical to the parable in Luke 19, as was pointed out earlier, they are similar in their overall theme and emphasis. Both are about a man who goes on a long journey and asks his slaves to invest his resources. Both focus on opportunities and reward, both involve an evaluation of three slaves, and in both parables the first two slaves are faithful while the final is unfaithful.

Matthew 25:24-30 identifies the third servant as an unbeliever who is cast into outer darkness:

> The one also who had received the one talent came up and said, "Master, I knew you to be a hard man, reaping where you did not sow and gathering where you scattered no seed. And I was afraid, and went away and hid your talent in the ground. See, you have what is yours." But his master answered and said to him, "You wicked, lazy slave, you knew that I reap where I did not sow and gather where I scattered no seed. Then you ought to have put my money in the bank, and on my arrival I would have received my money back with interest. Therefore take away the talent from him, and give it to the one who has the ten talents." For to everyone who has, more shall be given, and he will have an abundance; but from the one who does not have, even what he does have shall be taken away. Throw out the worthless slave into the outer darkness; in that place there will be weeping and gnashing of teeth.

Some commentators believe this third servant in Matthew 25 was a believer who was unfaithful to the Lord and will simply suffer loss of reward and joy. They believe that the outer darkness or "darkness outside" is simply the "reverse of the joy inside" and that "the unfaithful servant is excluded from that joy."[4]

To me that's a major stretch. Note this servant was cast into outer darkness, a place of weeping (suffering) and gnashing of teeth (despair). The words "outer darkness" appear three times—in Matthew 8:12; 22:13; and 25:30. In all three passages, the context points to the outer darkness as a synonym for hell or eternal separation from God.[5]

As John Walvoord said, "No Christian justified by faith and declared righteous by God could ever be cast into outer darkness."[6]

The parallels between the parables in Matthew 25 and Luke 19 support identifying the third slave in Luke 19 as a false follower of Jesus—someone who professes to know Him but does not possess Him.

Fourth, Jesus made clear that this servant didn't trust or know the nobleman. He desperately tried to excuse himself for not loving and serving him. "Another came, saying, 'Master, here is your mina, which I kept put away in a handkerchief; for I was afraid of you, because you are an exacting man; you take up what you did not lay down and reap what you did not sow'" (Luke 19:20-21).

The action taken by the third servant raises this question: Why did he hide his mina? Notice he offered a lame excuse. He said he hid it because he thought the master was harsh and exacting. If that were true, he had all the more reason not to bury it in the ground but to at least put it in the bank to draw interest. Putting the mina in the bank required minimal effort. As Chuck Swindoll said, "Drawing interest required no work from him and ran no risk of failure; therefore, he must have had another reason for sitting on the money."[7] The nobleman knew the slave's explanation was hollow, and, in essence, he responded, "You're lying."

So why didn't the third slave invest his mina? The reason for his inaction is simple—indifference. He cared nothing for the interests of the master. He didn't want to bother with the mina. Any effort to mess with the mina was too much. He was too involved with his own interests.

In contrast, the first two servants involved their whole lives in investing the resources and opportunities entrusted to them. They thought about their minas constantly, exploring ways to maximize the master's return. "The first two seized the opportunity to serve their Master in his absence; the third man took advantage of the Master's absence to pursue his own selfish ends."[8] He displayed a complete lack of concern about his master's business.

The hiding of the mina rather than putting it in the bank also raises another problem for the third servant. Evidently he did not believe the master was returning:

> The third servant...reasoned that his master might not be coming back at all. If he did return someday, the servant could simply return the talent to his master without loss from any poor investment (v. 25). But if he failed to return, the servant wanted to be able to keep the talent for himself. He did not want to deposit the talent in a bank where it would be recorded that the talent belonged to the master (v. 27). His reasoning indicated he lacked faith in his master.[9]

Referring to the third slave, John MacArthur notes, "He was careless, lazy, and thoughtless, and had no desire to honor or please his master. Instead of being motivated by love, he was driven by fear, and sought to defend himself by shifting blame to the king."[10]

New Testament scholar Darrell Bock says,

> The third servant represents people who are related to the king in that they are associated with the community and have responsibility in it. Nevertheless their attitude shows that they do not see God as gracious and that

they have not really trusted him. The third slave's attitude toward the master is important. He does not see his master as gracious, but as hard and unjust, and so he does not respond to the king...Such people are left with nothing at the judgment; they are sent to outer darkness, because they never really trusted or knew God...By his own attitude toward the master, the third servant is shown to not have had a real relationship with the master.[11]

The first two servants were faithful; the third servant was not.

Jesus's treatment of this man is instructive. He stripped away everything he had and gave it to the first servant. This is the ultimate "use it or lose it" story.

Jesus taught the sobering truth that *what you do with your mina ultimately reveals what you think of the Savior.* If you know Jesus and trust Him, you will at least invest your mina and work to maximize the return on it. If you don't know Him and trust Him, you will be indifferent and inactive. What each servant thought of the nobleman was revealed by what he did with the mina.

What about you? Are you so involved with your own business, education, possessions, friends, sports, and social life that you've buried the mina? Which servant are you like?

The Enemies

There's a final group here introduced in Luke 19:27—they are avowed enemies of the returning master. Of them Jesus said, "These enemies of mine, who did not want me to reign over them, bring them here and slay them in my presence." This pictures the terrible judgment that will be meted out when Jesus returns against all those who reject Him.

In this parable, Jesus proclaims the solemn truth that in the future, there are three groups of people who will be called to account.

There will be

> *rewards* for the faithful
> *rejection* for the false
> *retribution* for the foes

These are the only three groups that appear. That's it. There are no other categories. This embraces all of humanity. Every person will fall into one of these three groups. What group are you in?

The Significance

Many of the lessons from this parable have already been pointed out along the way, but I want to take a moment to review and reinforce the significance of this story. First, it teaches us the King is coming. The King has been away in heaven for a long time—2,000 years. But He is coming. His return is certain. And the kingdom is coming with Him.

This parable also teaches that while we are waiting for the *end time*, we must be investing our lives in the *meantime*. As we await the King's return, we're surrounded by investment opportunities. What are you doing with what you have? Are you bullish on the kingdom? Are you expending your efforts on the things that will last? What you do with time, money, and the gospel have eternal significance. What you do with your mina will define your life for eternity.

The lesson is simple: "Serve faithfully here, rule perfectly there."[12]

Christ expects a spiritual return—an increase—on His investment when He returns. Invest it. Work it. Manage it. Improve it. Maximize it. To the two faithful servants Jesus said, "Well done." He didn't say, "Well thought," "Well intended," or "Well planned." He said, "Well *done!*"

John MacArthur reminds us:

> Christ, the Master is coming soon. Opportunity slips away with each passing minute. When He returns, it

will be too late to recover lost opportunity. Everything we have belongs to Him. Faithfulness with the gifts and opportunities He has entrusted to us will bring staggering reward. Precious opportunities slip away with each passing moment. When Jesus comes it will be too late to recover lost opportunity...Now is our only time to prepare. Today is the only opportunity we are guaranteed.[13]

We are surrounded today by wonderful opportunities every day. Let's invest our mina and maximize the returns. Dr. S. Lewis Johnson said,

Trading with the riches of Jesus Christ is the highest and noblest enterprise in which a man could be involved. And each one of us has been given something by God with which we are to trade. Are you trading? Are you doing business for the Lord with the gifts that he has given you? Are you really actively seeking to honor him and glorify him in what you are doing? The time is coming when you shall stand before him as judge, and you shall hear either well done thou good and faithful servant, or some lesser accolade, or the opposite of wicked and slothful servant.[14]

The final hour may be upon us. The King is coming. May each of us invest and grow our mina faithfully so that when the Master comes we can hear those wonderful words, "Well done, My good and faithful servant."

CHAPTER EIGHT

Your Final Exam

*We'll have all eternity to celebrate our victories, but
only one short hour before sunset to win them.*

Robert Moffatt

Imagine you're in a high school classroom on a sunny Friday afternoon. You are daydreaming as you gaze out the window. Suddenly you snap back to reality as the teacher reminds the class that a major exam is on the schedule for Monday. The students let out a collective groan, but then everyone is elated when the teacher says she will give everyone the questions that will be on the test. Knowing the questions ahead of time will cut down the amount of time you'll need to study over the weekend. You get a pencil and, as the teacher states the questions, you write them down. What a great advantage! You know that you will have no excuse for doing poorly on the big test.

As we've seen so far in this book, Scripture teaches that there's a final exam on God's prophetic calendar for believers. It's not a pop quiz. The Lord has clearly announced that it's coming. It's in the

syllabus. It's on the schedule. He has even reminded us that it's coming. None of us should be caught by surprise when it arrives.

Moreover, not only has the Lord told us about the test, He has
graciously given us the test questions ahead of time. No believer will
be left to wonder what's on the test. There's no mystery about what
we need to know. The Lord has told us what He's looking for in our
lives in the final evaluation.

I've seen many lists of what the Lord will reward in our final
exam. Here's one of the more helpful ones.

1. Seeking Him through spiritual acts like fasting and prayer
   (Matthew 6:6; Hebrews 11:6)

2. Submitting to your employer (Colossians 3:22-24)

3. Self-denial (Matthew 16:24-27)

4. Serving people in need (Mark 9:41)

5. Suffering for His name (Matthew 5:11-12; Luke 6:22-23)

6. Sacrificing for Him (Matthew 19:29; Luke 6:35)

7. Sharing your time, talent, and treasure (1 Timothy 6:18-19)[1]

Actions God Rewards

As I've mined God's Word in the course of my own study, I've
identified fourteen types of actions in this life that God has promised to reward in the future. These are what the Lord will be looking
for when we stand before Him someday. These are the test questions; these are the things God rewards.

1. How We Treat Other Believers

The Lord will graciously reward us based on how we treated
other people here on earth, especially our fellow believers. Hebrews
6:10 says, "God is not unjust so as to forget your work and the love

which you have shown toward His name, in having ministered and in still ministering to the saints." God will never forget how we've treated His people, yet it's often a shame how believers treat their fellow brothers and sisters in Christ. The people we should love most and care about most deeply are often the objects of criticism, gossip, and unkindness. An old poem expresses this well:

> To live above,
> With saints we love,
> O, wouldn't that be glory.
> But to live below,
> With the saints I know,
> That's another story.

Let's not allow that to be true in our lives. Let's lovingly minister to the needs of God's people. He will never forget our labor of love.

2. How Generous We Are with Our Money

Concerning money, we've all heard the saying, "You can't take it with you!" You may have also heard someone say, "You never see a U-Haul behind a hearse." While it is true you can't take it with you, Jesus did say, "You can send it on ahead." Every person on earth is a steward of God's blessings. Everything we have belongs to Him. During our brief stay on Earth, we are given some of His assets to manage. How we manage them will follow us to heaven. "Store up for yourselves treasures in heaven, where neither moth nor rust destroys, and where thieves do not break in or steal; for where your treasure is, there your heart will be also" (Matthew 6:20-21).

The main focus of Matthew 6:19-24 is not renouncing our earthly treasures, but rather, the accumulating of heavenly treasures. You can't take it with you, but you can send it on ahead. Speaking of Moses, who looked for the heavenly reward (Hebrews 11:24-26), Tim Chester says,

The Egyptians locked up their treasures in the pyramids so that they could take them into the afterlife. But they couldn't. How do I know? Because I've seen their treasures in the British Museum. Moses, though, still has his reward.

"You can't take it with you," people say. Not true. You can take it with you. But first you must convert it into the currency of heaven and that currency is love and good works. You can take it with you by giving it away!…How do we lay up treasure in heaven? By being generous with earthly treasure.[2]

First Timothy 6:17-19 has this to say:

Instruct those who are rich in this present world not to be conceited or to fix their hope on the uncertainty of riches, but on God, who richly supplies us with all things to enjoy. Instruct them to do good, to be rich in good works, to be generous and ready to share, storing up for themselves the treasure of a good foundation for the future, so that they may take hold of that which is life indeed.

Giving to those in need is a specific area of sharing that the Lord promises to reward, as long as our motivation is right.

Beware of practicing your righteousness before men to be noticed by them; otherwise you have no reward with your Father who is in heaven. So when you give to the poor, do not sound a trumpet before you, as the hypocrites do in the synagogues and in the streets, so that they may be honored by men. Truly I say to you, they have their reward in full. But when you give to the poor, do not let your left hand know what your right hand is doing, so that your giving will be in secret; and your Father who sees what is done in secret will reward you (Matthew 6:1-4).

People today are always looking for safe places to invest their money. They consider stocks, bonds, treasuries, precious metals, and real estate. While each of those investments have their advantages on Earth depending on the economic climate, Jesus said that ultimately, there is only one safe place in which to invest: heaven.

Randy Alcorn says it well:

> Every day, the person whose treasure is on earth is headed away from his treasure. Every day, the person whose treasure is in heaven is headed toward his treasure. Whoever spends his life heading away from his treasure has reason to despair. Whoever spends his life headed toward his treasure has reason to rejoice. Where's your treasure? Are you heading toward it or away from it? Do you have reason to despair or reason to rejoice?[3]

You and I will be reviewed and rewarded for how we invested our resources in God's work. How much do you have in your account in heaven?

3. How We Support Others in Ministry

Jesus will reward us for our secondary involvement and influence through our support of the ministry of others:

> He who receives you receives Me, and he who receives Me receives Him who sent Me. He who receives a prophet in the name of a prophet shall receive a prophet's reward; and he who receives a righteous man in the name of a

> righteous man shall receive a righteous man's reward. And
> whoever in the name of a disciple gives to one of these lit-
> tle ones even a cup of cold water to drink, truly I say to
> you, he shall not lose his reward (Matthew 10:40-42).

This means if you support a church, local pastor, missionary, or
ministry by giving them money you will receive the same reward
they receive. When that missionary or minister receives his reward,
you will stand with him and participate in his reward. Jesus didn't
say you will receive part of his reward. He said you will get his
reward.

This means we should be intentional and thoughtful about
where we invest our resources. We need to make sure we plant our
giving in fertile soil that will bring a bountiful harvest. Support missionaries and ministries that are bearing fruit so you can receive a
full reward.

4. How Well We Accept Mistreatment and Injustice

In Matthew 5:11-12, Jesus said, "Blessed are you when people
insult you and persecute you, and falsely say all kinds of evil against
you because of Me. Rejoice and be glad, for your reward in heaven
is great; for in the same way they persecuted the prophets who were
before you."

If we suffer for our own foolishness or negligence, then that's on
us, but suffering for standing up for the truth brings reward. Our
culture today is turning more and more against Christianity. Believers are mocked, maligned, and marginalized with impunity. It's open
season on us. We're marked with a big bull's-eye. As we stand for
traditional marriage, life in the womb, and the exclusivity of Jesus
Christ as the way to God, we're fair game. This shouldn't surprise us.
Jesus told us repeatedly that we would suffer tribulation for His sake.
"You will be hated by all because of My name, but it is the one who
has endured to the end who will be saved" (Matthew 10:22).

In Luke 6:27-28, 35 Jesus tells us how to respond:

> I say to you who hear, love your enemies, do good to those who hate you, bless those who curse you, pray for those who mistreat you...love your enemies, and do good, and lend, expecting nothing in return; and your reward will be great, and you will be sons of the Most High; for He Himself is kind to ungrateful and evil men.

This takes the matter even further. Not only are we to endure the insults from today's culture, but we're to love unbelievers and do them good. Responding in this way brings great reward, according to Jesus. It's easy to get exasperated and angry in response to the pressure and persecution we face today, but we need more agonizing for the lost and less anger.

5. How We Endure Suffering and Trials

As with every test, some questions are more difficult than others. At the climax of the Beatitudes, Jesus revealed one of the more challenging points on the test we will face:

> Blessed are those who have been persecuted for the sake of righteousness, for theirs is the kingdom of heaven. Blessed are you when people insult you and persecute you, and falsely say all kinds of evil against you because of Me. Rejoice and be glad, for your reward in heaven is great; for in the same way they persecuted the prophets who were before you (Matthew 5:10-12).

Scripture also says, "Blessed is a man who perseveres under trial; for once he has been approved, he will receive the crown of life which the Lord has promised to those who love Him" (James 1:12).

"Do not fear what you are about to suffer. Behold, the devil is about to cast some of you into prison, so that you will be tested, and you will have tribulation for ten days. Be faithful until death, and I will give you the crown of life" (Revelation 2:10).

This part of our exam is not easy, but we can be thankful the Lord has revealed it to us so we can prepare for it. Patiently enduring and persevering in the dark valleys of life will bring the Lord's praise someday when you stand before Him.

6. How We Spend Our Time

The oldest psalm in Scripture (Psalm 90) was written by Moses. In verse 12, Moses wrote, "So teach us to number our days, that we may present to You a heart of wisdom." Expressing a similar thought about the preciousness of time, the apostle Paul says, "Making the most of your time, because the days are evil" (Ephesians 5:16). Every person has 168 hours to spend each week. Much of that time is spent sleeping and taking care of mundane yet necessary responsibilities, yet the Lord expects a return on the investment of our time. He expects us to make the most of the time He has given us. We need to count our days and make the most of them.

Thomas Chalmers, who lived in the late 1700s and early 1800s, was a minister in the Church of Scotland. In the early days of his pastorate, he did not know God and was not known for his godliness. He spent little time studying God's Word. He was a man without a passion for God or His Word and held a low view of the ministry. But all that changed dramatically when God got his attention through a broken engagement, serious illness, and the death of his sister and two brothers to tuberculosis. His life was turned upside down, and as a result, he came to faith in Christ. Gone were the lazy, wasted days of his earlier years in ministry. As a truly converted man and minister, he set about making Christ, His gospel, and His church his all-consuming pursuit. His newfound evangelical fervor stood in distinct contrast to his earlier years. Later in life, reflecting back on the time he had wasted, Chalmers said, "I had forgotten two magnitudes: I thought not of the littleness of time, and I recklessly thought not of the greatness of eternity."[4]

Time passes by each moment, and there's no way to retrieve it. We talk about saving time, making time, or borrowing time, but you can't do any of those things. As someone has said, "Remember, when you kill time, it has no resurrection." There's no time to waste. Once it's gone, you cannot get it back. Make sure you're making the most of every moment the Lord gives you.

7. How We Run the Race God Has Given Us

According to Scripture, each believer has a race to run. I have mine, and you have yours. Our responsibility is to run our race with endurance and stay in our lane. Hebrews 12:1 calls this "the race marked out for us" (NIV). We each have a lane to run in, and our races vary greatly. No two are the same. We each face our own set of challenges. As Kent Hughes reminds us,

> We each have a specific course mapped out for us, and the course for each runner is unique. Some are relatively straight, some are all turns, some seem all uphill, some are a flat hiking path. All are long but some are longer. But each of us can finish the race "marked out for us." I may not be able to run your course, and you may find mine impossible, but I can finish my race and you yours. Both of us can finish well if we choose and if we rely on him who is our strength and our guide.[5]

In 1 Corinthians 9:24, the apostle Paul said, "Do you not know that those who run in a race all run, but only one receives the prize? Run in such a way that you may win." In Philippians 3:14, he wrote, "I press on toward the goal for the prize of the upward call of God in Christ Jesus."

Hebrews 12:1 says, "Since we have so great a cloud of witnesses surrounding us, let us also lay aside every encumbrance and the sin which so easily entangles us, and let us run with endurance the race that is set before us."

I like Joe Stowell's humorous comments about running:

> I have nothing against runners. Some of my best friends are addicted runners. Though I have never seen a runner smiling, apparently there is something fulfilling about it. I even tried it once, waiting for that surge of ecstasy that my friends told me I would experience, only to find that the ecstasy came when I stopped running.[6]

Stowell continues:

> So, whatever you think about running, it's important to note that the Bible often speaks of living the Christian life as if we were running a race. Following Jesus is clearly more than a leisurely stroll in the park! And the issue is not whether you will run the race. When you became His follower, you were put in the race. The question is not *will* you run, but *how* will you run.[7]

William Wyler was the director of the original movie *Ben-Hur*. When work on the movie began, Wyler talked to Charlton Heston—the star who played the role of Judah Ben-Hur—about the all-important chariot race at the end of the movie. Wyler decided Heston should learn to drive the chariot himself rather than use a stunt double. That would make the race so much more realistic. Heston agreed to take chariot-driving lessons so the movie could be as authentic as possible. As you can imagine, learning to drive a chariot with four horses was no small matter. After extensive work and days of practice, Heston returned to the movie set and reported to Wyler, saying, "I think I can drive the chariot all right, William, but I'm not at all sure I can actually win the race." Smiling slightly, Wyler said, "Heston, you just stay in the race, and I'll make sure you win."

That's a great illustration of the spiritual race we're all running as Christians. Jesus says to us what Wyler said to Heston: "You just stay in the race, and I'll make sure you win." Throw off the encumbrances and entanglements, and run your race to win.

8. How Effectively We Control Our Body

We all face temptations of the flesh: sexual immorality, lust, and gluttony. How well we discipline our bodies and bring them under control is one of the test questions we must answer in this life.

> Do you not know that those who run in a race all run, but only one receives the prize? Run in such a way that you may win. Everyone who competes in the games exercises self-control in all things. They then do it to receive a perishable wreath, but we an imperishable. Therefore I run in such a way, as not without aim; I box in such a way, as not beating the air; but I discipline my body and make it my slave, so that, after I have preached to others, I myself will not be disqualified (1 Corinthians 9:24-27).

The same trait that makes a great athlete makes a faithful believer—discipline. That's not a popular word nowadays, but there's no substitute for old-fashioned self-control and self-discipline when it comes to sins of the flesh.

The Greek word translated "discipline" in verse 27 is a strong term from the boxing ring that literally means to "strike under the eye" or "make black and blue." The NIV translation reads: "I strike a blow to my body and make it my slave." The Phillips translation says, "I am my body's sternest master." We must be merciless to ourselves in bringing our bodies and desires under control and in conformity with God's will. This is radical stuff. We must spare no effort in disciplining ourselves and doing whatever it takes to run the race well. As Jesus said, "If your right eye makes you stumble, tear it out and throw it from you...If your right hand makes you stumble, cut it off and throw it from you" (Matthew 5:29-30). He wasn't saying to do those things literally, but rather, emphasizing the need to be strict with ourselves.

There's no substitute for discipline. We must rigidly apply ourselves daily by spending quality time in the Bible, in prayer, and in fellowship with God's people. We must avoid compromising situations that will increase the likelihood that we will fall into sin. The choice we face is stark—discipline now, or disqualification in the future. There are no other options.

9. How Many Souls We Witness to and Win for Christ

Every believer is called to be a faithful witness for Jesus Christ. We are His ambassadors to this world (2 Corinthians 5:20). Sharing the gospel with others and leading them to faith in Jesus brings us reward.

For the apostle Paul, the believers he led to Christ at Thessalonica were his reward. "Who is our hope or joy or crown of exultation? Is it not even you, in the presence of our Lord Jesus at His coming? For you are our glory and joy" (1 Thessalonians 2:19-20).

We all lack courage at times when it comes to sharing our faith. We need to pray earnestly for opportunities and boldness to share the good news with lost people around us. Our responsibility is to proclaim the gospel, and it is the Holy Spirit who does the work of convicting and winning unbelievers. Only He can open a human heart. Our job is simply tell others the good news, and to tell it simply.

10. How Faithfully We Look for Christ's Coming

The second coming of Jesus Christ is mentioned more than 300 times in the 260 chapters of the New Testament—that comes out to one of every thirty verses. Jesus Himself referred to His second coming at least twenty-one times. People are exhorted more than fifty times to be ready for the return of Jesus Christ.

Looking for Christ's coming and preparing for it by living a godly life will bring reward to us. He is looking for people who are looking for Him. The apostle Paul lived with this attitude of expectancy: "In the future there is laid up for me the crown of righteousness, which the Lord, the righteous Judge, will award to me on that day; and not only to me, but also to all who have loved His appearing" (2 Timothy 4:8).

Jesus admonished us:

> Be dressed in readiness, and keep your lamps lit. Be like men who are waiting for their master when he returns from the wedding feast, so that they may immediately open the door to him when he comes and knocks. Blessed are those slaves whom the master will find on the alert when he comes; truly I say to you, that he will gird himself to serve, and have them recline at the table, and will come up and wait on them. Whether he comes in the second watch, or even in the third, and finds them so, blessed are those slaves (Luke 12:35-38).

Those who are watching, ready and alert, will be blessed by Jesus. At some point every day this thought should pass through our minds: *Perhaps today.* Today may be the day when Jesus comes. Living with the blessed hope burning in our hearts and minds will motivate us to live a godly life, qualifying us for the crown of righteousness.

11. How Passionately We Pray

Robert Murray McCheyne, the famous Scottish pastor, said, "You wish to humble a man? Ask him about his prayer life."[8] We can all relate to struggling over our prayer life. Prayer is hard, humbling work. A lot of what we do in the Christian life is easier than prayer.

In His famous Sermon on the Mount, Jesus called His followers to persistent prayer with a pure heart with the promise of reward.

> When you pray, you are not to be like the hypocrites; for they love to stand and pray in the synagogues and on the street corners so that they may be seen by men. Truly I say to you, they have their reward in full. But you, when you pray, go into your inner room, close your door and pray to your Father who is in secret, and your Father who sees what is done in secret will reward you (Matthew 6:5-6).

As always, motives matter. "We are rewarded by the person whose praise we seek."[9] Devoted prayer done in secret will be rewarded by the Lord when He comes.

12. How Hospitable We Are to Strangers

The New Testament word translated "hospitality" (Greek, *philoxenia*) means "a lover or friend of strangers." We are to reach out and show friendship to strangers. Hospitality is a subset of love and calls us to open our hearts and homes to others. Yet we all know that showing true hospitality is not easy. Hospitality can be a burden. It can be costly, messy, irritating, time-consuming, and requires effort and planning. It interrupts our privacy. Then there's the clean-up work we have to do afterward.

In *Poor Richard's Almanack*, Benjamin Franklin wrote that fish and guests are the same—they both start to stink after three days. Donald Coggan, the former Archbishop of Canterbury, said, "True hospitality is making people feel at home, while you wish they were at home."[10] Every believer in Christ is charged to "be hospitable to one another without complaint" (1 Peter 4:9).

The early church used their home in remarkably effective and gracious ways. Resist the temptation of thinking you are too "introverted" for hospitality. This really has nothing to do with personality types, or whether or not you enjoy having company over for dinner. We must see it as a biblical pattern, practiced among all types of God's people—who have all types of personalities...Following Jesus includes following His practice of hospitality—joyous authentic, generous, countercultural, and hope-filled hospitality...opening up our homes and lives to others...You don't need a bigger TV and a more comfortable recliner in your "man-cave." You need a bigger front door, and more seats filled around the table.[11]

Showing hospitality to strangers and those in need may not seem like much in the larger scheme of life, yet the Lord highly honors hospitality. Jesus said,

> When you give a luncheon or a dinner, do not invite your friends or your brothers or your relatives or rich neighbors, otherwise they may also invite you in return and that will be your repayment. But when you give a reception, invite the poor, the crippled, the lame, the blind, and you will be blessed, since they do not have the means to repay you; for you will be repaid at the resurrection of the righteous (Luke 14:12-14).

Jesus isn't saying we can't invite our friends, family, or the wealthy to our home; He is saying don't invite *only* them. He's saying we need to reach out to the needy and disenfranchised as well.

Far too often what we do for others is done with a view toward receiving something back for ourselves. We help out a friend, expecting they will return the favor. We host a wealthy, influential person for lunch or dinner hoping for some return or repayment or the prestige we will get from being seen with that person. Jesus said the most valuable kind of giving and entertaining is that which helps those who cannot respond to us in kind, and hospitality is something everyone can do. Max Lucado says,

> Long before the church had pulpits and baptisteries, she had kitchens and dinner tables. Even a casual reading of the NT unveils the house as the primary tool of the church. The primary gathering place of the church was the home. Not everyone can serve in a foreign land, lead a relief effort, or volunteer at the downtown soup kitchen. But who can't be hospitable? Do you have a front door? A table? Chairs? Bread and meat for sandwiches? Congratulations! You just qualified to serve in the most ancient of ministries: hospitality.
>
> Something holy happens around a dinner table that will never happen in a sanctuary. In a church auditorium you see the backs of heads. Around the table you see the expressions on faces. In the auditorium one person speaks; around the table everyone has a voice. Church services are on the clock. Around the table there is time to talk. When you open your door to someone, you are sending this message: "You matter to me and to God." You may think you are saying, "Come over for a visit." But what your guest hears is, "I'm worth the effort."[12]

How hospitable are you? With neighbors? With people at your church? With foreign students at the local college or university? With those in need?

Never forget—Jesus promises to honor the hospitable.

13. How Faithful We Are in Our Vocation

If you are an adult with a full-time job, then you are spending more time in your occupation than in any other endeavor. The manner in which you fulfill the responsibilities of your job can bring rewards in the future.

> Slaves, in all things obey those who are your masters on earth, not with external service, as those who merely please men, but with sincerity of heart, fearing the Lord. Whatever you do, do your work heartily, as for the Lord rather than for men, knowing that from the Lord you will receive the reward of the inheritance. It is the Lord Christ whom you serve (Colossians 3:22-24).

The time you spend at your job every day is not inconsequential. It's not throwaway time. It carries spiritual and eternal consequences. How you do your work will be reviewed by the Lord and rewarded where appropriate.

When the famous pastor H.A. Ironside was a boy, he worked for a shoe repairman named Dan MacKay. Dan was a devoted believer in Christ who desired to bring glory to God through his work. Young Harry's job was the monotonous task of pounding the water out of soaked pieces of cowhide for shoe soles. One of MacKay's unscrupulous competitors down the street eliminated the process of pounding the water out of the soles. This saved time during the shoemaking process, but it also meant the customer would have to come back sooner for a repair. Harry didn't understand why MacKay went to all the trouble of removing water out of the soles, but MacKay's response was unwavering.

"Harry," he said, "I do not cobble shoes just for the [money] I get from my customers. I am doing this for the glory of God. I expect to see every shoe I have ever repaired in a big pile at the judgment seat of Christ, and I do not want the Lord to say to me on that day,

'Dan, this was a poor job, you did not do your best here.' I want Him to be able to say, 'Well done, good and faithful servant.'"

Then MacKay went on to explain that just as some men are called to preach, so he was called to fix shoes, and that only as he did this well would his testimony count for God. Reflecting on those words, Ironside said:

> It was a lesson I have never been able to forget. Often when I have been tempted to carelessness, and to slip-shod effort, I have thought of dear, devoted Dan MacKay, and it has stirred me up to seek to do all for Him who died to redeem me.[13]

All of us will give an account to God for our work someday. I'm a pastor, and I think about all my sermons there in a pile at the judgment seat. Maybe you're an attorney, a mechanic, a physician, a geologist, an accountant, an IT expert, a housewife, or an electrician. Expect to see all your work piled at the judgment seat to be evaluated by the Lord. Maybe it will be a pile of legal briefs, medical records, diapers, laundry, computer programs, or repaired automobiles. Whatever you do, make sure you'll be happy to see it again in the presence of your Master.

Ben Patterson shares the remarkable story of a B-17 bomber that was returning from a bombing mission in the waning days of World War II.

> The plane was hit several times by shells and flak, with some of the hits directly into the fuel tank. Miraculously, the bomber did not explode. When it landed, eleven unexploded twenty-millimeter shells were taken out of the fuel tank! The shells were dismantled, and to the amazement of everyone, all were empty of explosives. Inside one shell was a note written in Czech. Translated,

it read, "This is all we can do for you now." A member of the Czech underground, working in a German munitions factory, had omitted the explosives in at least eleven of the twenty-millimeter shells on his assembly line.[14]

Patterson concludes:

> That worker must have wondered often if the quiet (and dangerous) work he was doing to subvert the Nazi war effort was going to make any difference whatsoever to the outcome of the war. He may have died wondering. So it is with our work. We may not see now the place in God's plan that our work as a secretary or waiter or telephone repair worker occupies. But his promise that work done in the Lord is not in vain fortifies us against despair.[15]

How you do your work now will determine the nature of your work forever.

14. How Humble We Are

Jesus said humility will be greatly rewarded. "Whoever then humbles himself as this child, he is the greatest in the kingdom of heaven" (Matthew 18:4). Humility is a beautiful virtue every believer should desire, yet it's a slippery one to possess because as the saying goes, the moment you begin to think you have it, you've lost it. Humility is elusive.

We all know humility when we see it, but being a truly humble person isn't easy. How do we become humble? The secret is this: "Humble yourselves in the presence of the Lord, and He will exalt you" (James 5:10). It's in the presence of God that we humble ourselves. Seeing who He is in creation and in the Bible gives us a proper view of who we are. The famous preacher Phillips Brooks provided this recipe for humility: "The true way to be humble is not to stoop until you are smaller than yourself, but to stand at your real height against some higher nature that will show you what the real smallness of your greatness is."[16] When we stand next to the greatness of God, we will gain a true estimation of ourselves. As the Puritan John Flavel said, "They that know God will be humble, and they that know themselves cannot be proud."

Another sure way to cultivate humility is to never stray too far from the foot of the cross. The cross reveals our desperate need for forgiveness and our spiritual bankruptcy apart from Christ. It reminds us that we have nothing in our hands to bring to Christ. We must cling to Christ alone for salvation. Humble yourself every day in the presence of God and at the foot of the cross.

When He comes, Jesus will give great honor to the humble.

Keep the Date

The final exam is coming. If you know the Lord, you'll be there, and so will I. We can't call in sick. We don't get to repeat the exam. There's no second chance. There's no makeup test. There's no grading on the curve. You get only one shot.

Now is your opportunity to prepare and get ready. You have the questions. Start studying now. Don't wait until the last minute to cram for the test. You and I have no excuse to fail. Let's commit to do all we can every day to ace the test, to get an *A* so we can hear those words, "Well done, My good and faithful servant."

CHAPTER NINE

Your Ultimate Payday

*Five minutes after we die every Christian will
understand that heaven is our home and earth was
simply a temporary lodging on the homeward journey.
Then we'll know for certain what was important and
what wasn't. We will see with eternity's clarity. We
will know exactly how we should have lived.*[1]

Randy Alcorn

In the summer of 2018, basketball all-star Lebron James inked a four-season $154 million deal with the Los Angeles Lakers. Broken down, that means he will earn $38,500,000 per season, $498,512 per game, $117,378 per quarter, $9,781 per minute, $163 per second. That doesn't take into consideration the money he receives from endorsements and other sources.

Very, very few people can relate to the kind of payday Lebron experiences. Still, whatever it is we make, we love payday. For some of us, it's once a week, for others, it's biweekly, and for still others, it's once a month. However often it occurs, it's an important day for us, one that is often circled on the calendar.

Between paydays, bills accumulate, finances fade, things break, and excitement wanes. But when payday comes, we experience relief. And if you're waiting on a bonus, overtime pay, or a nice commission, the anticipation is heightened. Let's face it—few days are like payday.[2]

While we all look forward to our weekly or monthly paydays, most of us probably give little thought to the greatest payday of all. On that day, every previous payday will pale in comparison—even Lebron's. This payday will eclipse them all.

Jesus told a fascinating parable about the coming payday for God's people.

> The kingdom of heaven is like a landowner who went out early in the morning to hire laborers for his vineyard. When he had agreed with the laborers for a denarius for the day, he sent them into his vineyard. And he went out about the third hour and saw others standing idle in the market place; and to those he said, "You also go into the vineyard, and whatever is right I will give you." And so they went. Again he went out about the sixth and the ninth hour, and did the same thing. And about the eleventh hour he went out and found others standing around; and he said to them, "Why have you been standing here idle all day long?" They said to him, "Because no one hired us." He said to them, "You go into the vineyard too."
>
> When evening came, the owner of the vineyard said to his foreman, "Call the laborers and pay them their wages, beginning with the last group to the first." When those hired about the eleventh hour came, each one received a denarius. When those hired first came, they thought that they would receive more; but each of them also received a denarius. When they received it, they grumbled at the landowner, saying, "These last men have worked only one hour, and you have made

them equal to us who have borne the burden and the scorching heat of the day." But he answered and said to one of them, "Friend, I am doing you no wrong; did you not agree with me for a denarius? Take what is yours and go, but I wish to give to this last man the same as to you. Is it not lawful for me to do what I wish with what is my own? Or is your eye envious because I am generous?" So the last shall be first, and the first last (Matthew 19:27–20:16).

As you read the parable, you may have been thinking to yourself, *This seems patently unfair. How can the owner pay all these workers the same amount? It's bad business. Labor unions would boycott this vineyard.* Yet Jesus said God is like this when He pays His people.

This passage gives us the principles of God's payroll—principles of God's reward program.

The Principles of God's Reward Program

As we unpack this parable, I want us to gather our thoughts around three simple points:

1. The Promises—the Setting
2. The Parable—the Story
3. The Principles—the Significance

Let's begin with the setting.

The Promises—the Setting

We will never fully understand this parable unless we back up a few verses into Matthew 19 to get the setting. Context is always important when studying any passage of Scripture, and it's especially critical when interpreting parables. Context is king.

In Matthew 19, Jesus challenged a rich young ruler to leave everything he had and follow Him to have treasure in heaven.

> Someone came to Him and said, "Teacher, what good thing shall I do that I may obtain eternal life?" And He said to him, "Why are you asking Me about what is good? There is only One who is good; but if you wish to enter into life, keep the commandments." Then he said to Him, "Which ones?" And Jesus said, "You shall not commit murder; you shall not commit adultery; you shall not steal; you shall not bear false witness; honor your father and mother; and you shall love your neighbor as yourself." The young man said to Him, "All these things I have kept; what am I still lacking?" Jesus said to him, "If you wish to be complete, go and sell your possessions and give to the poor, and you will have treasure in heaven; and come, follow Me." But when the young man heard this statement, he went away grieving; for he was one who owned much property.
>
> And Jesus said to His disciples, "Truly I say to you, it is hard for a rich man to enter the kingdom of heaven. Again I say to you, it is easier for a camel to go through the eye of a needle, than for a rich man to enter the kingdom of God." When the disciples heard this, they were very astonished and said, "Then who can be saved?" And looking at them Jesus said to them, "With people this is impossible, but with God all things are possible" (Matthew 19:16-26).

The next verse, Matthew 19:27, begins with the word "Then." Peter asked Jesus a probing question that was triggered by the interaction that had just happened with the rich young ruler.

> Then Peter said to Him, "Behold, we have left every-
> thing and followed You; what then will there be for us?"
> And Jesus said to them, "Truly I say to you, that you who
> have followed Me, in the regeneration when the Son of
> Man will sit on His glorious throne, you also shall sit
> upon twelve thrones, judging the twelve tribes of Israel.
> And everyone who has left houses or brothers or sisters
> or father or mother or children or farms for My name's
> sake, will receive many times as much, and will inherit
> eternal life. But many who are first will be last; and the
> last, first" (Matthew 19:27-30).

Peter, sometimes known as "the American apostle," wanted to
know what he was going to get for his sacrificial service for the Lord.
His question is understandable in light of all the sacrifice he had made.
Unlike the rich young ruler, Peter and the other disciples had left
everything to follow Jesus. Peter wanted to know, "What then will
there be for us?" In a sense he was asking, "How much will we get?"

Remember in the preceding context how the rich young ruler
responded? What was his attitude? Bargaining. He haggled with
Jesus about what he had to do to obtain eternal life. What did Peter
do? He caught the bargaining spirit. He wanted to cut his deal with
the Lord. In the original Greek text, the phrase "for us" is emphatic.
Peter said, "*For us*, what will there be?"

Now before we rebuke Peter, let's remember what he gave up to
follow Jesus. He left his home, his wife (at least temporarily), and
his lucrative family fishing business. He truly gave up everything.

To answer Peter's query and correct his attitude, the Lord told a
parable. Before He began, He gave Peter a wonderful promise. He
told Peter that this world would one day be regenerated or born
again. This world is suffering birth pains today. Everywhere we look
we see suffering as well as natural disasters—such as tornadoes, vol-
canoes, earthquakes, and hurricanes. But a new age is coming. Jesus

spoke of the coming millennium, or 1,000-year kingdom of Christ on Earth. He spoke of a literal future earthly kingdom for Israel as prophesied in the Old Testament. The apostles never forgot this promise that they would one day sit on twelve thrones and judge the twelve tribes of Israel. After Jesus ascended to heaven in Acts 1, the first order of business among the apostles was to select a new apostle to occupy the spot vacated by Judas.

Jesus proceeded to tell Peter that every sacrifice for His sake would be greatly rewarded both in this life and the next. "Everyone who has left houses or brothers or sisters or father or mother or children or farms for My name's sake, will receive many times as much, and will inherit eternal life" (Matthew 19:29). Jesus was referring to the spiritual family we inherit upon entering our relationship with Him. Doug McIntosh says,

> If you decide to go on a missions trip for two weeks, you will find that the family you left behind, whom you miss so terribly, is partly compensated for by the people you spend time with on the trip. Your fellow missionaries become dear to you because you are serving Christ together. At the same time, you find that the house you left behind has been replaced by a dozen houses in the place to which you go, thanks to the courtesy of like-minded pilgrims...The deeper your commitment to the age to come, the less you feel deprived of anything you lose in this age.[3]

That's the promise. That's the setting. It does pay to serve the Lord. It really is worth the effort and sacrifice. In fact, it more than pays.

But there is a caution that Jesus gives in a parable in Matthew 20.

The Parable—the Story

The parable in Matthew 20 is bracketed by two parallel statements given in opposite order:

Many who are the first will be last; and the last, first (Matthew 19:30).

The last shall be first, and the first last (Matthew 20:16).

This literary device is known as an inclusio, which is similar to bookends or brackets that concentrate the focus on what lies between the two bookends. In this case, Jesus inverted the saying for emphasis. With these bookends, Jesus was alerting us that there will be major surprises when God gives out our "payment," or rewards.

There are two main parts to the parable:

1. The *Hiring* of the Workers
2. The *Paying* of the Workers

The Hiring of the Workers

The scene Jesus painted would have been a familiar one to His listeners. It was one that was played out repeatedly during harvest season. Laborers would gather in the town marketplace early in the morning (6:00 a.m.), and landowners would come by to secure the necessary retinue of workers for the day. The typical work day was twelve hours long (from 6:00 a.m. to 6:00 p.m.), with two hours of rest during the day for meals and prayer.

In Jesus's story, a vineyard owner shows up in the marketplace at 6:00 in the morning to recruit workers for the grape harvest. In Israel, grapes ripen near the end of September. After that, the rain begins to fall. There is a short window of only about two weeks when grapes could be harvested. Extra help was often needed to harvest the produce quickly. The harvest was a frantic race against time, and any available worker was welcome. This vineyard owner needed all the help he could find, so he went back to the marketplace multiple times throughout the day to hire more workers. He returned at 9:00 a.m., 12:00 noon, 3:00 p.m., and 5:00 p.m. These five sets of hires were divided into two groups based on how they were hired. What we want to pay attention to is *how* the workers were hired.

The 6:00 a.m. workers (the early birds) were hired with a contract. "A landowner...went out early in the morning to hire laborers for his vineyard. When he had agreed with the laborers for a denarius for the day, he sent them into his vineyard" (Matthew 20:2). They struck their bargain before they were hired. These all-day workers cut their deal for one denarius for one day's work. The word "agreed" in verse 2 is the Greek word *symphonia*, which refers to a meeting of the minds.

Remember the context—Jesus's encounter with the rich young ruler and Peter had happened prior to this. Just like them, the 6:00 a.m. workers in the parable bargained before going to work. They wanted to be certain of what they would get.

All the other workers who were hired that day went without a contract.

At 9:00 a.m., the landowner "saw others standing idle in the market place; and to those he said, 'You also go into the vineyard, and whatever is right I will give you.' And so they went" (verses 3-4). Notice these workers simply trusted the owner's word and character to give them what was right. There was no bargaining.

The owner needed more workers, so he hired another group at 12:00 p.m. More workers were brought to the field at 3:00 p.m., and yet another group was employed at 5:00 p.m., one hour before quitting time. These other groups also agreed to work for whatever the owner would pay them.

The Paying of the Workers

In that culture, payday happened every day. At the end of the day, at sunset (around 6:00 p.m.), workers would line up to be paid. In Jesus's story, the vineyard owner began by paying the last group first. This was in keeping with the parable's principle that the last will be first and the first will be last.

Each worker in the five o'clock group, who had labored for only one hour, was given a denarius, which in that day was the going rate for a full day of work. Then the landowner paid the 3:00, 12:00, and 9:00 groups a denarius each.

As this scene is unfolding, we can only imagine what was going through the minds of the six o'clock hires—those who had worked all day. They must have been recalculating, in their minds, the amount of pay they would receive as the owner went down the line. At first they couldn't wait for their turn. If the group that had worked for only one hour had gotten a full denarius, then surely they would receive a bonanza. Yet as they realized the other groups were all being paid the same amount, they must have become deflated. Sure enough, when it was their turn, the landowner dropped a bombshell. To their utter astonishment, he paid each of them a denarius as well.

Immediately they complained and grumbled (verse 11). In response, the vineyard owner turned to one of them and said, "Friend, I am doing you no wrong; did you not agree with me for a denarius?...Is it not lawful for me to do what I wish with what is my own?" (verses 13, 15). The employer told the early birds they had been given exactly what they had bargained for—one denarius for one day's work. The owner then dismissed them rather abruptly.

Matthew 20:15—"Is it not lawful for me to do what I wish with what is my own?"—has been called the golden verse of capitalism. An owner can do as he pleases with what he owns.

What principles do we learn from this parable? What spiritual truths does the Lord want us to learn about our coming payday?

The Principles—the Significance

There are three views about the main point of this parable.

First, some believe this parable teaches that it's not the quantity of the work one does for the Lord that matters, but the quality. This view holds that the last group of workers received as much as the all-day group because they labored harder. The problem with this view is that there's nothing in the parable to indicate that is the case. The vineyard owner never mentioned the quality of anyone's work. He did not congratulate the final group for their diligence while chiding the six o'clock laborers for their sloth.

Second, others maintain that everyone will receive the same reward in heaven. They say this refers to the reward of our salvation—all God's people will receive a denarius, which represents eternal life. Those who support this view point out that Jesus, in the preceding passage, had discussed eternal life with the rich young ruler. They cite Matthew 19:29, which refers to inheriting "eternal life."[4] Every believer, no matter how immature, disobedient, or weak, has the same prospect of inheriting the kingdom. While this view is biblical, I don't believe it's what this parable is about.

Third—which I believe is the best explanation—the parable teaches God's principles of rewards, or how He pays His people in the afterlife. Whatever this parable means, it must be connected to the immediately preceding context, where Peter asked Jesus about rewards in the coming kingdom. The nearest context of the parable focuses on final rewards, not salvation.

With this understanding serving as the backdrop, I see in this story eight key principles about future rewards.

1. Length of service does not determine the degree of reward

The Lord pays based on our faithfulness with the opportunity given to us, not the amount of time we serve Him. People "clock in" at different times. Some become Christians early in life. Others receive Christ as Savior in their twenties or thirties. Still others do so late in life. This parable is a powerful antidote to discouragement for those who become saved near the end of life. Length of service does not determine the degree of reward.

I'm an all-day worker if there ever was one. I can't remember a time when I didn't know and accept that Christ died for my sins. I became saved a month before I turned six while watching a Billy Graham crusade on television.

This means I have had the opportunity to serve Christ all my life. Not that I've always done it, but I've had the chance. In the parable, Jesus taught that rewards are based on faithfulness to the opportunity given. God is sovereign and all-knowing. He has the ability to take every factor into consideration, including length of service and what we've been entrusted with. Notice in Matthew 20:6 that the landowner asked the eleventh-hour workers, "Why have you been standing here idle all day?" Their sad reply was, "Because no one hired us" (verse 7). In other words, they had no opportunity.

This last group of hires depicts those who come to Christ later in life and have less time to serve Him. Jesus graciously assures us that length of service does not determine the degree of reward. This is great news for those who come to Christ late in their lifetime, possibly even at the last hour.

From the time you enter the vineyard, seize the opportunities you are given and make the most of the time the Lord has given you.

2. Position does not determine the degree of reward

The Gospel of Matthew was written primarily to a Jewish audience. His focus was on proving that Jesus was the promised King of the Jews. However, all through the book, Matthew highlighted Gentiles and their acceptance of Jesus. We first see this in the story of the wise men, who came from a distant land to worship Jesus. There's a great deal of interplay in Matthew between the Jewish rejection and Gentile reception of Jesus.

As we consider the Jews and Gentiles in relation to Jesus's parable, we need to ask: Who had the contract with God? The answer, of course, is the Jewish people. They had the covenant with God— the Law of Moses. Because of this, the Jewish people often believed they had special status before God. They are the six o'clock workers.

The length of their service was a source of pride. These workers represent the Jews, yet Jesus said the Gentiles who were brought in later were on equal footing when it came to rewards. This shocked the Jews.

This same idea applies to every believer's position in the church as well. No one has a higher status than anyone else. Don't get caught up in your position and think that because of it you will receive a greater reward. Pastors, missionaries, elders, and teachers don't have a leg up on everyone else. In fact, those who teach God's Word will face a more strenuous examination (James 3:1).

Position does not determine the degree of reward.

3. God is sovereign with regard to giving rewards

In Matthew 20:15, the owner of the vineyard responded bluntly to the complaints of the all-day workers: "Is it not lawful for me to do what I wish with what is my own?" The point Jesus made is that kingdom rewards depend on God's sovereign act. It's His vineyard. He does as He pleases. He owns it all and bestows rewards sovereignly.

The same truth was emphasized a few verses later when Jesus responded to the mother of James and John when she asked if her two sons could sit on Jesus's right and left sides in the coming kingdom. Jesus said, "My cup you shall drink; but to sit on My right and on My left, this is not Mine to give, but it is for those for whom it has been prepared by My Father" (verse 23).

The message is clear in both passages: God is the sovereign one. He owns it all. It's His vineyard. No one can rightfully challenge how He chooses to grant rewards. He will evaluate all the circumstances of each believer's life and give what is right. He sees us and sees through us.

This reminds me a humorous tale I heard years ago. Children were lined up for lunch in the cafeteria of a Catholic elementary school. At the head of the table was a large pile of apples. After watching them for a while, the supervising nun wrote a sign and posted it on the apple tray:

"Take only ONE. God is watching!"

The children kept moving further along in line, and at the other end of the table was a large pile of chocolate chip cookies. One of the children looked at the cookies, then wrote a sign that read: "Take all you want. God is watching the apples."

The truth is that God is watching the cookies as well as the apples. He knows and sees all. He will give to each of His children what is right. No one can question how He chooses to disperse His rewards.

4. *God is generous in giving rewards*

The workers who were hired at five o'clock received a full day's wages for one hour of labor. What a deal! The Lord is the best boss you could ever have. He owes us nothing—in fact, we deserve eternal punishment for our sins. He didn't have to bring us into His vineyard in the first place. He didn't have to come to the marketplace to hire anyone.

The same is true for us. God is under no obligation to bring us into His vineyard to begin with. Salvation is purely by God's grace. But for His calling on our life and giving us the gift of faith, we would never even be in His vineyard. His generosity is overwhelming. As Erwin Lutzer notes,

> We are rewarded because of His generosity, not His obligation...Think this through: God gives us the faith by which we believe in Christ, and yet for this faith He gives us the gift of eternal life. God then works within us so that we might serve Him, and for our service He honors us with eternal rewards or privileges. Of course we don't deserve those rewards! But we are the sons and daughters of a loving Father who is more benevolent than we could possibly expect Him to be. He delights in giving to those who do not deserve His love.[5]

The vineyard owner is lavish when it comes to giving rewards.

5. Beware of watching other workers

The parable of the workers in the vineyard strikes at the heart of our idea of fairness. The all-day laborers complained, "These last men have worked only one hour, and you have made them equal to us who have borne the burden and the scorching heat of the day" (verse 12).

Most of us have entertained thoughts like these at one time or another. Filled with envy, we wonder why so-and-so is getting more than us when he hasn't served the Lord as faithfully as we have or sacrificed as much.

The apostle Peter struggled with focusing on the lot of others in life. After Jesus told Peter how he would die, the disciple pointed to his friend John and asked, "What about him?" Jesus's response was classic: "Follow Me." Jesus told Peter, "Don't worry about what John will get; you follow Me" (see John 21:18-22). Jesus says the same to us.

When it comes to rewards, we must guard against the curses of comparison and envy. A recent experiment revealed how even animals want to get a fair shake.

> Monkeys were taught in an experiment to hand over pebbles in exchange for cucumber slices. They were happy with this deal. Then the researcher randomly offered one monkey—in sight of a second—an even better deal: a grape for a pebble. Monkeys love grapes, so this fellow was thrilled. The researcher then returned to the second monkey, but presented just a cucumber for the pebble. Now, this offer was insulting. In some cases the monkey would throw the cucumber back at the primatologist in disgust. In other words, the monkeys cared deeply about fairness. What mattered to them was not just what they received but also what others got.

The article then looked at an example involving humans and drove the point home:

> Monkeys aren't the only primates instinctively offended by inequality. For example, two scholars examined data from millions of flights to identify what factors resulted in "air-rage" incidents. One huge factor: a first-class cabin. An incident in a coach section was four times as likely if the plane also had a first-class cabin; a first-class section increased the risk of a disturbance as much as a nine-hour delay did. When there is a first-class section, it is at the front of the plane and economy passengers typically walk through it to reach their seats, but in some flights the boarding is in the middle of the plane. The researchers found that an air-rage incident in coach was three times as likely when economy passengers had to walk through first class compared with when they bypassed it.[6]

Rather than wondering why others have what they have and get what they get, we should be amazed that we receive anything. We must not allow ourselves to be distracted by what happens to others.

After serving as a missionary for 40 years in Africa, Henry C. Morrison became sick and had to return to America. As the great ocean liner docked in New York Harbor, there was a large crowd gathered to welcome home another passenger on that boat. Morrison watched as President Theodore Roosevelt received a grand welcome-home party after his African safari. Resentment seized Henry Morrison and he turned to God in anger. "I have come back home after all this time and service to the church and there is no one, not even one person, here to welcome me home."

Then a still, small voice spoke to Morrison and said, "Henry—you're not home yet."[7]

The same is true for us. We're not home yet. Don't be distracted by what happens to others. Follow Jesus.

6. Beware of overconfidence

As the workers line up to receive their pay and the 5:00 group received a full day's pay, the all-day workers grew overconfident, even arrogant, that they would receive more. "When those hired first came, they thought that they would receive more; but each of them also received a denarius" (Matthew 20:10).

The lesson here is simple. Those saved early in life can grow over-confident about how they will be rewarded. Don't let that happen to you.

George Whitefield and John Wesley disagreed strongly, even vehemently, on some theological matters. However, they eventually learned to respect one another. When one of Whitefield's followers asked him if he thought he would see Wesley in heaven, Whitefield replied, "I fear not, for he will be so near the eternal throne and we at such a distance, we shall hardly get sight of him."[8]

May we emulate this gracious attitude when to comes to other believers and how God might reward them.

7. There will be many surprises in heaven when the Lord gives His rewards

I mentioned earlier that this parable is bracketed by the same words stated in reverse order.

- "Many who are first will be last; and the last, first" (Matthew 19:30).

- "The last shall be first, and the first last" (Matthew 20:16).

These bookends serve as a clue that the believers' payday will be filled with surprises. The rewarding of God's people will be filled with revelations and reversals. As Leslie Flynn says, "At the judgment seat of Christ when awards are given, some will receive real prizes, and some will get surprises."[9]

There's a story I like that, though it's not theologically precise, drives home a powerful point. After a preacher died and went to heaven, he noticed that a New York cabdriver had been given a greater reward than he had. "I don't understand," he complained to Peter. "I devoted my entire life to my congregation."

Peter said, "Our policy is to reward results. Whenever you preached, people fell asleep. When people rode in his taxi, they prayed."

God's payday will be filled with many shockers.

There's a legend about an angel who announced at the beginning of a church construction project that he would award a prize to the person who made the greatest contribution to the effort. Everyone wondered who would win—the architect, the contractor, the glass craftsman who assembled the beautiful stained-glass windows, or the carpenter who built the stunning woodwork. All labored diligently. The surprise winner was an elderly peasant woman who carried hay every day to the oxen that pulled the stones for the stonecutters.[10]

Let this truth encourage you in your service for the Lord: Most of us toil in routine, unglamorous, mundane work for Christ. Don't ever fall into the trap of thinking your service is unimportant or irrelevant. The issue is not whether we are famous or prominent. Rather, God desires that we be faithful.

The last will be first.

8. *Beware of making bargains with God*

The rich young ruler, Peter, and the six o'clock workers in the parable all made bargains; they cut their deals. They wanted to know what they had to do and how much they would get.

Who were the losers? The bargainers—those who insisted on a contract.

Who were the winners? Those who went out and served and trusted the landowner to pay them whatever was right.

Are you willing to serve the Lord without a contract? So many believers today make deals with God. "Make me rich, and I'll give back ten percent. Give me success. Give me..."

Why not just trust the Lord? If you let Him reward you as He sees fit, you'll receive more than you can ever imagine.

There's a story about a little boy who accompanied his father to a store. After the father had paid for his purchase, the clerk invited the child to help himself to a handful of candy. The youngster held back.

"What's the matter? Don't you like candy?" asked the clerk.

The child nodded, and smilingly, the clerk put his hand into the jar and dropped a generous portion into the little boy's pockets. Afterward, the father asked his son why he hadn't taken some candy when the clerk first invited him to. "Because his hand is bigger than mine," replied the boy.

That's the way God is. His hand is bigger than ours. He will always do more for us than we can conceive—if we leave the choice with Him.

Don't Miss the Point

The message of this parable is clear. There's a vineyard out there, and the Lord is saying, "It's My vineyard; I own it. Go work in it. Don't bargain and haggle; don't worry about the pay. Don't compare yourself to others. Instead, trust Me. I will reward you beyond your wildest imagination. I'll always give you much more than you're worth."

What a way to live!

What a Boss! What a Savior!

CHAPTER TEN

The Grand Bargain

*When I die I shall then have my greatest grief and
my greatest joy—my greatest grief that I have
done so little for Jesus, and my greatest
joy that Jesus has done so much for me.*[1]

William Grimshaw

The Shackleton Expedition has taken its place among the epic tales of human survival. The story begins when the Antarctic explorer Sir Ernest Shackleton ran an ad in a London newspaper, *The Times*, in the early part of the twentieth century—an ad that has become one of the most famous in history.[2]

> Men wanted for hazardous journey. Small wages, bitter cold, long months of complete darkness, constant danger, safe return doubtful.

As unappealing and unpleasant as that sounds, the response was overwhelming. Inquiries poured in, and as hard as it is to believe, the trip ended up being even worse than advertised.

Shackleton and his crew set sail in August 1915 and headed for a journey across the Antarctic land mass. Disaster didn't take long to strike. By October, their ship, the *Endurance*, became trapped in shifting ice floes. Eventually it began to break up under the crushing pressure of the ice.

Shackleton and his men abandoned ship and set up temporary camps on a series of ice floes. After several months, land was spotted on the distant horizon, and they took off in three small lifeboats. Seven harrowing days later, they came ashore on Elephant Island, which they discovered wasn't much better than the ice floes.

Desperate, Shackleton embarked on another longer and more dangerous journey to South Georgia Island with just one boat, the *James Caird*, and six men. The rest of the crew was left behind on the inhospitable wasteland of Elephant Island, waiting for Shackleton to return.

The journey to South Georgia Island was difficult. It covered 720 nautical miles in frigid waters. They believed the trip could take up to four months, but they made it in seventeen days in seas that repeatedly threatened to capsize their twenty-foot lifeboat, including a hurricane that sank a 500-ton steamer.

Eventually Shackleton returned to Elephant Island to retrieve his crew members who had stayed there. Incredibly, by the time the ordeal was over, Shackleton had not lost one single man.

The question that persists is this: Why would anyone want to volunteer for a voyage like the one advertised by Shackleton? Who in their right mind would want to earn low wages and live in bitter cold and constant danger?[3] As Ben Patterson notes, "That's what they signed up for; that's what they wanted. To travel with Shackleton would be the hardest challenge they ever faced. But hardship and danger were small prices to pay if it meant seeing something of the splendors of God, hearing the voice of nature, and reaching the naked soul of men. They were glory seekers. They thought the high price was a bargain."[4]

Earlier, when I quoted the ad that appeared in the London paper, I left out the last line—and did so on purpose. Here's the full ad:

> Men wanted for hazardous journey. Small wages, bitter cold, long months of complete darkness, constant danger, safe return doubtful. *Honour and recognition in event of success.*

That last line changed it all. The reason men couldn't sign up fast enough is that they were glory seekers. They thought the high price of self-sacrifice was a bargain. They were looking to the reward.

> Read only from the hardship angle, that statement is a turnoff; why go on a journey that is hard, hazardous, and dark? Read from the perspective of the glories of the journey's end, it's an altogether different matter; the path, though hard and narrow, leads to delights and glories in God's Kingdom that far outweigh whatever it costs to get there. The high price is really a bargain.[5]

The same is true for us. Salvation is a free gift, but the cost of discipleship is high. There's nothing cheap about coming to Christ. He calls us to deny ourselves, take up our cross, and follow Him (Mark 8:34). The cost is high, but the bargain of our heavenly rewards is greater still no matter what the cost. God will reward our service and sacrifice far beyond our ability to imagine. Eternal life, which is a free gift, is the ultimate prize, but our heavenly rewards for following Jesus faithfully will make our earthly sacrifices seem like nothing. Receiving eternal life as a free gift, serving the Lord on Earth, and then receiving extraordinary heavenly rewards for our meager efforts is the most stupendous, grandest bargain of all time. It seems too good to be true, yet this is precisely what the Bible teaches.

Here is the sequence:

- God gives us the faith to believe.
- God gives us the free gift of eternal life.
- God gives us the Holy Spirit and the grace and power to live for Him.
- God then gives us remarkable rewards in heaven for what He has graciously produced in and through us.

Our great God does it all for us, in us, and through us—to the praise of His glory.

It all begins by accepting Christ—by receiving the full pardon for all your sins, a pardon purchased by the death and resurrection of Jesus. All who receive Jesus become His children by faith (John 1:12).

Why not receive Him now if you've never done so? Why not sign up for the grand adventure of following Christ? All you have to do is *admit* you're a sinner, *acknowledge* you can't do anything to save yourself, and *accept* Jesus Christ as your substitute and Savior from sin. Call upon the Lord, and He promises He will save you (Romans 10:13).

The moment you receive Him you can begin to live for Him, putting His interests first in your life. You can begin to store up treasure in heaven and accumulate rewards that will affect your life forever. There is "honor and recognition in event of success."

A Fair Point

Tony Evans is a powerful preacher and compelling illustrator of biblical truth. He relates this story that puts a practical capstone on the topic of heavenly rewards.

> Every year in Dallas, the Texas State Fair comes to visit. This is fair heaven. There is more food than you could ever eat out there. Usually, I can go to the fair for free because

a member of the church will give me tickets. Like salvation, my entrance into this heavenly place is free. I receive a free gift that gains me entrance.

Now, inside the fairgrounds, there is so much to do...The best part is the Midway. This is where all the fun rides and roller coasters are. It's also where most of the games are. When you play games at the fair, it ends up costing you more to play the game than to buy whatever it is that you are attempting to win. It's all part of the fun though.

All of these various activities and events are available to me simply because I have entered the fair. Entrance to the fair gives me access to a lot of things.

The free ticket gains me entrance, but it does not automatically make me a full participant. All of the extra things available to me at the fair are like rewards. I can only enjoy them as much as I can afford them. I will have had to put in some work somewhere on somebody's job in order to be able to afford the additional fun that the fair offers.

Salvation is the free ticket available to those who accept Jesus Christ as their Savior. It guarantees free entrance into heaven. However, the amount we are able to enjoy heavenly rewards is tied to the amount of effort we've made on earth. Our heavenly rewards are tied to our earthly effort.[6]

Every believer will be at the fair, but how we live there and what we do there is being determined now by how we live and act each day.

That's the main thesis this book has sought to develop. Every believer has one shot at life, and our one shot will someday be reviewed and rewarded by the Lord. Our life in eternity will be determined by that accounting. What you do now has an irreversible effect on your eternity. There are permanent repercussions for what you do, think, and say every day and the *why* behind it all.

The life you live today will determine your life in eternity.

Take dead aim with your one shot and make it count!

Answers to a Few More Questions

What are the future judgments in Scripture?

The Judgment Seat of Christ is one of seven future judgments on God's prophetic calendar.

Seven Future Judgments

Judgment	Time	Scripture
Judgment Seat of Christ for church-age believers	Between the rapture and the second coming	1 Cor 4:5; 2 Cor 5:10
Old Testament saints	End of tribulation/ second coming	Dan 12:1-3
Tribulation saints	End of tribulation/ second coming	Rev 20:4-6
Living Jews	End of tribulation/ second coming	Ezek 20:34-38
Living Gentiles	End of tribulation/ second coming	Matt 25:31-46
Satan and fallen angels	End of the millennium	Rev 20:10
Unsaved people	End of the millennium	Rev 20:11-15

Will everyone be punished the same in hell?

This question is the logical and biblical counterpart to the truth about rewards in heaven. The Bible reveals that God is holy, just, and righteous; therefore, the punishment of sinners must be tailored to fit the crime. The Bible teaches that just as there will be varying degrees of reward for believers in heaven, there will be degrees of punishment in hell for unbelievers based on the amount and nature of the sins committed and the light that was refused. All unbelievers will go to the same place. They will all be consigned to the lake of fire, but Jesus Himself taught in at least three places in the Gospels that there will be degrees or gradations of punishment in hell.

> Truly I say to you, it will be more tolerable for the land of Sodom and Gomorrah in the day of judgment than for that city (Matthew 10:15).

> He began to denounce the cities in which most of His miracles were done, because they did not repent. "Woe to you, Chorazin! Woe to you, Bethsaida! For if the miracles had occurred in Tyre and Sidon which occurred in you, they would have repented long ago in sackcloth and ashes. Nevertheless I say to you, it will be more tolerable for Tyre and Sidon in the day of judgment than for you. And you, Capernaum, will not be exalted to heaven, will you? You will descend to Hades; for if the miracles had occurred in Sodom which occurred in you, it would have remained to this day. Nevertheless I say to you that it will be more tolerable for the land of Sodom in the day of judgment, than for you" (Matthew 11:20-24).

> The master of that slave will come on a day when he does not expect him and at an hour he does not know, and

will cut him in pieces, and assign him a place with the unbelievers. And that slave who knew his master's will and did not get ready or act in accord with his will, will receive many lashes, but the one who did not know it, and committed deeds worthy of a flogging, will receive but few. From everyone who had been given much, much will be required; and to whom they entrusted much, of him they will ask all the more (Luke 12:46-48).

These passages clearly reveal that some unbelievers will receive greater measures of punishment in the afterlife, and others lesser. These varying portions of punishment announced by the Lord will be meted out at the final great assize known as the Great White Throne Judgment.

I saw a great white throne and Him who sat upon it, from whose presence earth and heaven fled away, and no place was found for them. And I saw the dead, the great and the small, standing before the throne, and books were opened; and another book was opened, which is the book of life; and the dead were judged from the things which were written in the books according to their deeds. And the sea gave up the dead which were in it, and death and Hades gave up the dead which were in them; and they were judged, every one of them according to their deeds. And death and Hades were thrown into the lake of fire. This is the second death, the lake of fire. And if anyone's name was not found written in the book of life, he was thrown into the lake of fire (Revelation 20:11-15).

At the Great White Throne Judgment, all the lost from all the ages will be summoned by God to appear before His almighty bar of justice. No unbeliever will escape. No one's case can be postponed or dismissed on a technicality. All who appear at this judgment will be declared guilty, and all will be given a life sentence—or more accurately, an eternal death sentence of separation from God. Yet the severity of people's conditions will vary. Warren Wiersbe said, "The White Throne Judgment will be nothing like our modern court cases. At the White Throne, there will be a Judge but no jury, a prosecution but no defense, a sentence but no appeal. No one will be able to defend himself or accuse God or unrighteousness."[1]

At the Great White Throne Judgment, the Lord will open "books" and "another book" (Revelation 20:11-12). Based on the context of this passage and the rest of Scripture, it seems clear that the "book" (singular) is the Lamb's book of life that contains the names of all God's elect down through the ages. No one whose name appears in the book will be at the Great White Throne Judgment.

The "books" (plural) contain the names and all the works of the lost. From these books the Lord will mete out punishments that fit the crime. Nothing people have done will escape the all-seeing eye of God. Lady Justice in America is pictured as a blindfolded woman with a set of scales in her hand, symbolizing her impartiality as she dispenses justice. In contrast, the eternal God will judge with His eyes wide open.[2] He knows all, and He is fair. The degree of punishment He gives will vary from person to person.

> The books are thrown wide open and the past is recalled. Details long since forgotten are brought to light. The good, the bad, and the ugly. Many have a litany of good deeds: acts of charity, love, and sacrifice...Their good works will be carefully recounted, but none will be enough for admittance into heaven. But the good deeds done will make their punishment in the lake of fire more bearable. They will be judged on the basis of what they

did with what they knew, or should have known; thus hell will not be the same for everyone.[3]

One sobering fact we learn from this judgment is that hell is earned. As Scripture says, "The wages of sin is death" (Romans 6:23). We all deserve to go there. Heaven is the free gift of God to all who will receive Christ's pardon. The only reason any of us will ever make it to heaven is because of the matchless grace of Jesus.

Do people become angels in heaven as a reward?

The older I get, the more I find myself taking time each morning to quickly peruse the obituary page in our local newspaper. Several times over the years I've noticed statements to the effect that the person who has just died has become one of "God's angels." We've all seen the cartoons of a heavenly scene with a person bearing angelic wings on his back, strumming a harp, sitting on a cloud. For some reason, people seem to be comforted by the thought that their loved ones, especially children who die young, become angels when they get to heaven. Others have the idea that becoming an angel might be a special reward in heaven.

The Bible assumes the existence of angels from Genesis to Revelation. They are presented in Scripture as created beings. They can manifest themselves in human form, and in some Bible accounts, we are told they were mistaken for men. Interestingly, they never appear in female form. At least some ranks of angels do have wings, such as the seraphim described in Isaiah 6:2 (see also Revelation 4:8).

Angels and humans are similar in several ways: (1) both are servants of God, (2) both are immortal—that is, they will live forever, and (3) both have personality (mind, will, and emotions). Even with these similarities, the Bible makes it clear that angels are angels, and humans are humans. We are two totally different orders of beings. While humans possess a spirit, we are also creatures of flesh and bone. Angels are not. While they can assume human flesh and carry out human functions such as eating and drinking (Genesis 18:1-8), still, people do not become angels in heaven.

The mistaken notion that people become angels when they die is sometimes drawn from a misunderstanding of two statements made by Jesus:

- "In the resurrection they neither marry nor are given in marriage, but are like angels in heaven" (Matthew 22:30).
- "When they rise from the dead, they neither marry nor are given in marriage, but are like angels in heaven" (Mark 12:25).

The phrase "like angels in heaven" is often misconstrued to teach that people become angels in heaven. Context is always key, and we must notice that in these texts, Jesus was dealing with the subject of marriage. Angels were never given the command by God to be fruitful and multiply. They have no marital relationships and no ability to procreate. Jesus's point in these verses is that in heaven, people will no longer procreate. The mandate to be fruitful and multiply is limited to life on Earth. Heaven will be different. There, we will have a glorified body that will be infinitely different from the earthly one we have now. In heaven, we will *be like* angels in that one aspect—no more ability to procreate. But we will not *become* angels.

Four key points in Scripture confirm that believers do not become angels at death. First, there are marked differences between angels and humans. Angels are individual creations of God, while humans are a race. When Satan sinned against God and fell, each angel had a choice whether to join in the rebellion, and one-third made the disastrous decision to join the mutiny (Revelation 12:3-4). But when Adam, the head of the human race, fell into sin, he took us all with him (Romans 5:12). We had no choice. In Adam, all humans fell.

Second, redeemed human beings will one day judge the angels

(1 Corinthians 6:3). In this present life we are a little lower than the angels, but in the life to come we will be over them (Psalm 8:5; Hebrews 2:7). If we will judge the angels, then we must be distinct from them.

Third, Luke 16:22 says angels came and carried the soul of Lazarus, the poor beggar, to Paradise, to Abraham's bosom. If humans transition to angelic beings at death or as a reward, why would we need angels to come carry us into the presence of the Lord?

Fourth, there are two New Testament passages that distinguish redeemed people from angels in heaven.

One is Hebrews 12:22-23:

> You have come to Mount Zion and to the city of the living God, the heavenly Jerusalem, and to myriads of angels, to the general assembly and church of the firstborn who are enrolled in heaven, and to God, the Judge of all, and to the spirits of righteous men made perfect, and to Jesus, the mediator of a new covenant, and to the sprinkled blood, which speaks better than the blood of Abel.

This passage lists all the inhabitants of heaven. Note that angels and the church of the firstborn (believers in the present church age) are distinct from each other. Old Testament saints are referred to as "the spirits of righteous men made perfect," and they too are distinguished from angels.

The second text that clearly distinguishes angels and humans in heaven is Revelation 5:11:

> I looked, and I heard the voice of many angels around the throne and the living creatures and the elders; and the number of them was myriads of myriads, and thousands of thousands.

The "elders" is a reference to the twenty-four elders who are mentioned twelve times in the book of Revelation. I believe these elders are symbolic of the church in heaven. The angels in heaven and these elders are mentioned separately, indicating that they aren't the same beings.

One of our rewards in heaven is not becoming an angel but judging the angels. As the bride of Christ, our place in heaven will be above the angels. We will be second only to the Lord in the order and authority of His unshakeable kingdom.

Will we know each other in heaven, and know the rewards others receive?

Every person who believes in heaven has probably asked these questions at one time or another. I've been asked these many times. We want to know whether we will recognize our friends and loved ones, and whether they will know us. And we also wonder if we know the rewards that others receive in heaven.

Scripture is clear that we will not only see our friends and loved ones in heaven, we will know them. In fact, we could say that we won't really know each other *until* we get to heaven. Only in the perfection and righteousness of heaven, when all the masks and facades are torn away, will we truly know one another and enjoy intimate, unhindered fellowship.

The primary passage that indicates we will recognize each other in heaven is Luke 16:19-31. There, Jesus relates the parable of the rich man and a destitute beggar named Lazarus. They both die, with the rich man going to Hades and Lazarus to Abraham's bosom. In Hades, the rich man gazes into heaven, recognizes Lazarus, and remembers all the facts about their relationship on Earth. The rich man even remembers he has five brothers who are still on Earth.

Scripture also seems to indicate we will recognize people we never met here on Earth. At the transfiguration of Jesus, Peter instantly recognized the two men who were with Jesus—Elijah and Moses (Matthew 17:1-4). Obviously, Peter had never met them. How did he know who they were? It appears that he had an intuitive knowledge that enabled him to know.

I believe this is a preview of heaven, where all believers will possess an intuitive knowledge that will enable them to recognize their friends and loved ones as well as the redeemed of all the ages. I believe we will also know the rewards others receive. The giving of rewards will be public, so if we know each other, it makes sense that we will know the rewards given to others. I will know your rewards, and you will know mine. And there won't be any jealousy toward one another based on this knowledge. We will rejoice together in God's grace and goodness, and we will know that God's judgments are perfect and right.

Together, we will be eternally happy in the generosity of our Savior.

The Church Rewarded

The material below is excerpted, with permission, from Dr. John F. Walvoord's book *The Church in Prophecy*, originally published in 1964. I first read this book in the fall of 1985, and it had a seminal influence on my thinking about the future of the church and the reality of heavenly rewards.

I like to keep the words of my teachers and mentors from a past era before a new generation of God's people. This excerpt reinforces much of what I've written in this book, but also fills in a few additional details. I believe it's beneficial to hear similar truth expressed in various voices.

I hope this excerpt blesses you as much as it has blessed me over the years.

The Church Rewarded

One of the major features of the period during which the church is in heaven is the distribution of rewards for faithful service to the church at the judgment seat of Christ in II Corinthians 5:9-11. The fact of this judgment is declared to the Corinthian church:

"Wherefore we labour, that, whether present or absent, we may be accepted of him, for we must all appear before the judgment seat of Christ; that every one may receive the things done in his body, according to that he hath done, whether it be good or bad. Knowing therefore the terror of the Lord, we persuade men; but we are made manifest unto God; and I trust also are made manifest in your consciences."

Here, as many other times in the Pauline letters, the church is challenged to labor for Christ in view of the necessity of ultimately giving account to the Lord after He comes for His own. It is a judgment which relates to Christians only and has to do with the matter of rewards for faithful service. Paul declares in II Corinthians 5:9 that this is a worthy motive for labor for Christ that "we may be accepted of him," or better translated, "that we may be well pleasing to him." The fact is stated that all Christians must appear before the judgment seat of Christ that they may receive a just recompense for what they have done in life. The basis of the judgment will be whether their deeds were good or bad.

It should be clear from the general doctrine of justification by faith and the fact that the believer is the object of the grace of God that this is not an occasion in which the believers are punished for their sins. All who are in Christ Jesus are declared to have "no condemnation" (Romans 8:1). It is a question of sorting out the good from the bad, the bad being discarded but the good being subject to reward. Paul mentions, however, in II Corinthians 5:11 that he is impelled by "the terror of the Lord" to continue in his task of persuading men to believe and serve the Lord. The terror which Paul mentions is not that of the possibility of being lost or unsaved, but rather the terror of coming before his Lord with a wasted life. In that day, when grace has brought him to the privileged place of being with the Lord in heaven, the thought of having to present a life that has not been properly spent in the Lord's service fills him with terror. It was this fear that drove him on in his service for the Lord.

The truth of the judgment seat of Christ, declared in its main principles in II Corinthians 5, is presented elsewhere in the Pauline letters under three different figures. One of the basic presentations is that of the believer's life as a stewardship. The child of God is pictured as having been entrusted with a responsibility which he must discharge on behalf of his master. On the basis of this stewardship, believers are exhorted not to judge others but rather to judge themselves. In Romans 14:10-12 this truth is presented, "But why dost thou judge thy brother? or why dost thou set at nought thy brother? for we shall all stand before the judgment seat of Christ. For it is written, As I live, saith the Lord, every knee shall bow to me, and every tongue shall confess to God. So then every one of us shall give account of himself to God."

Inasmuch as each believer must give account to God, it is presumptive for a believer to attempt to judge his brother especially in areas where doubt exists as to what the will of God may be. This does not mean that the preacher of the Gospel is not called upon to rebuke sin or to reprove those who are outside the will of God, but it does require a recognition of the fact that our judgment is not the final one. Ultimately our main question is not whether someone else is serving the Lord, but whether we ourselves are properly fulfilling God's stewardship as committed to us. The principle is plainly laid down, however, in verse 12, that everyone will have to account for his life at the judgment seat of Christ.

The thought of stewardship is reinforced and given further explanation in I Corinthians 4:1-5, "Let a man so account of us, as of the ministers of Christ, and stewards of the mysteries of God. Moreover it is required in stewards, that a man be found faithful. But with me it is a very small thing that I should be judged of you, or of man's judgment: yea, I judge not mine own self. For I know nothing by myself; yet am I not hereby justified: but he that judgeth me is the Lord. Therefore judge nothing before the time, until the Lord come, who both will bring to light the hidden things of darkness, and will make manifest the counsels of the hearts: and then shall every man have praise of God."

Here the Christian is especially reminded that he is a steward of the truth of God and that as such he is required to be found faithful. As in the Romans 14 passage, it is made clear that the main issue is not what man may think about it as there are limitations in our evaluation of our own life. Paul states that the Lord Himself is going to judge him and that therefore we should not attempt to evaluate our stewardship prior to that time. In judging the stewardship of a believer, God not only examines the act itself but the hidden motive and counsels of the heart which prompted it. Paul concludes with a note of expectation, "Then shall every man have praise of God."

A second important figure is used relative to the judgment seat of Christ in picturing the believer's life as a building built upon the foundation which is Christ. In I Corinthians 3:11-15, the foundation is described as already laid, which is Jesus Christ. Upon this foundation, each man is called to build a building or a life which will stand the test of God's final judgment. Paul writes the Corinthians: "Now if any man build upon this foundation gold, silver, precious stones, wood, hay, stubble; every man's work shall be made manifest: for the day shall declare it, because it shall be revealed by fire; and the fire shall try every man's work of what sort it is. If any man's work abide which he hath built thereupon, he shall receive a reward. If any man's work shall be burned, he shall suffer loss: but he himself shall be saved; yet so as by fire" (I Corinthians 3:12-15).

In using the figure of a building, attention is called first of all to the fact that it must be built on the proper foundation, namely, salvation in Christ. Everyone who appears at the judgment seat of Christ will meet this qualification as a person who has put his trust in Christ and has been accepted in the Beloved. Upon the foundation of our salvation in Christ, it is necessary for us to erect our lives. The materials mentioned are typical of what may be incorporated. The gold, silver, and precious stones represent that which is precious and indestructible, whereas the wood, hay, and stubble represent that which is unworthy and subject to destruction. As the passage makes plain, the building will be tested by fire and that which abides after it is tested by fire, namely, the gold, silver, and precious stones which by their nature are fireproof, are going to be made the basis for reward. Christians are assured, however, that even if their building be burned, they will be saved as far as their eternal destiny is concerned but they will be stripped of reward. This is stated in I Corinthians 3:15, "If any man's work shall be burned, he shall suffer loss: but he himself shall be saved; yet so as by fire." Comparing this to I Corinthians 4:15, it seems evident that every Christian will have something commendable about his life, but relatively speaking some will have a life mostly wasted, composed of wood, hay, and stubble, in contrast to those who have lived for eternal things as represented in gold, silver, and precious stones.

Many suggestions have been made concerning the typical meaning of these six building elements. The wood, hay, and stubble clearly represent three degrees of worthlessness as far as eternal values are concerned. Wood obviously is the best construction of the three and may represent temporary things in our life of a necessary nature as scaffolding in the construction of a building. However, when tested by fire the wood is destroyed even though it may be constructed well and be beautiful in its appearance. Hay represents that which is much more transitory, useful for animals but not fit for human consumption. Stubble represents that which is completely worthless. All alike, however, are reduced to ashes.

By contrast, the gold, silver, and precious stones, though much smaller in size and more difficult to obtain, are able to survive the fire. Gold in Scripture is typical of the glory of God and the perfection of His attributes and may represent that in our lives which is Christlike or which reveals the perfection of God's handiwork and grace. Silver is characteristically the metal of redemption and may speak of personal evangelism and of efforts in the extension of the

Gospel. Precious stones are not identified and probably purposely are not related to any particular stone. This seems to refer to all other works of God manifest in the life of believers offering a great variety of beauty and color and illustrating that believers may serve the Lord in many different ways. The gold, silver, and precious stones, however, have this one important characteristic, that they are able to survive in the fire.

Taken as a whole, the figure of a building is a reminder, first, of the necessity of building upon Christ the foundation as the only true preparation for eternity. Second, our lives should be lived in such a way that they will have eternal value, and the time and effort extended will be worthy of reward by the Lord at the judgment seat of Christ. It is a reminder that the only real values in life are those which are eternal.

A third figure representing the issues raised at the judgment seat of Christ is used in I Corinthians 9:24-27 where the believer's life is compared to the running of a race or of contending in a fight. The apostle writes: "Know ye not that they which run in a race run all, but one receiveth the prize? So run, that ye may obtain. And every man that striveth for the mastery is temperate in all things. Now they do it to obtain a corruptible crown; but we an incorruptible. I therefore so run, not as uncertainly; so fight I, not as one that beateth the air: but I keep under my body, and bring it into subjection: lest that by any means, when I have preached to others, I myself should be a castaway."

According to this passage, the objective in running the race of life is to receive the prize from the Lord at the end of the race. We are to be guided in our life by this objective. Just as an athlete must apply self-discipline and be self-controlled in all areas in order to win the race, so also the Christian must make all things conform to the ultimate goal of pleasing the Lord at the judgment seat of Christ. Competing athletes, as Paul reminds us, do this to obtain a corruptible crown, that is, a crown of laurel leaves such as were commonly given at the races in Greece. By contrast, the Christian is looking forward to an incorruptible crown, that is, a crown which will not decay quickly like a crown of leaves.

With this incentive, the apostle declares that he himself runs not in an uncertain manner and that he fights not as one that is simply going through the motions. Instead he keeps under his body, literally, "beats it black and blue," thereby bringing it into subjection to his will. The apostle fears that having preached to others to dedicate their lives to the Lord and serve Him, he himself may be a castaway or one who is disapproved or disqualified. The reference to being disapproved does not relate to salvation, but to reward. It is a picture of an athlete who by breaking the rules is disqualified from winning the race. The figure makes plain that a Christian should bend all his efforts to living in such a way that he will not be ashamed when his life is reviewed at the judgment seat of Christ.

The concept of winning a crown or a victor's wreath at the end of the race is spoken of elsewhere in the Scriptures. In II Timothy 4:8, the Apostle Paul declares, "Henceforth there is laid up for me a crown of righteousness, which the Lord, the righteous judge, shall give me at that day: and not to me only, but unto all them also that love his appearing." Here the reward is viewed in a general way as recognizing Paul's righteous life at the judgment seat of Christ symbolized in the victor's crown. Paul does not claim to have a peculiar right to such recognition but declares instead that a similar crown will be given to all who love the appearing of Christ.

The eternal life which will be the possession of all true believers is likewise called a crown in James 1:12 and Revelation 2:10. James writes, "Blessed is the man that endureth temptation: for when he is tried, he shall receive the crown of life, which the Lord hath promised to them that love him" (James 1:12). This passage does not teach that some Christians will have life and others will not, but rather that the very possession of eternal life and its enjoyment in heaven is one of the forms of compensation which the believer will have for his life of service on earth, even though it is based upon the grace of God and the sacrifice of Christ rather than upon his own attainment. The same is true of the mention in Revelation 2:10 where the promise is given to the faithful martyrs, "I will give thee a crown of life." Those who suffer a martyr's death will all the more enjoy the freedom in glory of life in heaven which is their heritage.

The idea of a crown as a symbol of reward is also mentioned in I Peter 5:4 where the statement is made, "And when the chief Shepherd shall appear, ye shall receive a crown of glory that fadeth not away." The crown which is a symbol of reward is described here as a crown of glory that does not fade away, and in I Corinthians 9:25 it is mentioned as an incorruptible crown. It will be a glorious day for the saints when the Lord rewards His own. Their recognition will not be transitory like the successes of this life, but will continue forever.

The various crowns mentioned in Scripture taken together are a symbolic representation of the recognition by Christ of the faithful service of those who put their trust in Him. II John 8 adds a word of exhortation, "Look to yourselves, that we lose not those things which we have wrought, but that we receive a full reward." While salvation is entirely by grace, rewards are related to faithfulness in Christian testimony and it is possible for the Christian to fall short of the reward that might have been his. Though there is a just recognition of attainment in faith and life, the saints in glory will nevertheless recognize that it is all of grace and that apart from redemption in Christ Jesus their works would have been unacceptable before God. This is brought out in the worship of the four and twenty elders in Revelation 4:10 who cast their crowns before the throne and say: "Thou art worthy, O Lord, to receive glory and honour and power: for thou hast created all things, and for thy pleasure they are and were created" (Revelation 4:11). If the four and twenty elders represent the church, as many believe, the fact that they are rewarded at this point in the book of Revelation is another indication that the church will be in glory following the rapture and translation while the tribulation unfolds in scenes of earth.

The final triumph of the church in relation to being in heaven with Christ will come at the time of His second coming to the earth when the church will accompany Him to the earth. Some find reference to this in I Thessalonians 3:13 in the phrase, "at the coming of our Lord Jesus Christ with all his saints." This phrase, however, may refer to the arrival of the church in heaven rather than the return of the church to the earth. More specific is Jude 14, where the prediction is recorded, "Behold, the Lord cometh with ten thousands of his saints." The church may well be numbered with the armies of heaven mentioned in Revelation 19:14 in the triumphal return of Christ to put down the wicked and to claim the earth which is rightfully His. In view of the imminent return of Christ, the prospect of the glory of the church in heaven is an ever-present one to saints of this generation, and the events which now are prophecy may become a reality very suddenly. Prophecies relating to the church in heaven, however, are only the beginning of a sequence of events which will carry the church into the eternal state.

Recommended Books for Further Study on Heavenly Rewards

Alcorn, Randy. *The Law of Rewards: Giving What You Can't Keep to Gain What You Can't Lose*. Carol Stream, IL: Tyndale House Publishers, 2003.

Benware, Paul. *The Believer's Payday: Why Standing Before Christ Should Be Our Greatest Moment*. Chattanooga, TN: AMG Publishers, 2002.

Epp, Theodore H. *Present Labor and Future Rewards*. Lincoln, NE: Back to the Bible, 1960.

Hoyt, Samuel H. *The Judgment Seat of Christ: A Biblical and Theological Study*. Milwaukee, WI: Grace Gospel Press, 2011.

Ironside, H.A. *Salvation and Reward: Two Distinct Lines of Truth*. Reprint. Ross-Shire, Solid Christian Books, 2015.

Kendall, R.T. *The Judgment Seat of Christ*. Ross-Shire, Scotland: Christian Focus, 2004.

Woodrow Kroll. *Facing Your Final Job Review: The Judgment Seat of Christ, Salvation, and Eternal Rewards*. Wheaton, IL: Crossway Books, 2008.

Lutzer, Erwin W. *Your Eternal Reward: Tears and Triumph at the Judgment Seat of Christ*. Chicago, IL: Moody Press, 1998.

Jones, Mark. *A Christian's Pocket Guide to Good Works and Rewards*. Ross-Shire, Scotland: Christian Focus, 2017.

Wall, Joe. *Going for the Gold: Reward and Loss at the Judgment of Believers*. Chicago, IL: Moody Press, 1991.

Wilkinson, Bruce. *A Life God Rewards: Why Everything You Do Today Matters Forever*. Colorado Springs, CO: Multnomah, 2002.

Notes

Foreward by Greg Laurie

1. Mark Hitchcock, *Heavenly Rewards* (Eugene, OR: Harvest House Publishers, 2019), 12.

2. Warren Wiersbe, *Being a Child of God* (Nashville, TN: Thomas Nelson, 1996) 9.

Chapter 1—One Shot

1. C.T. Studd, as cited in Nathan Busenitz, "Only One Life," June 24, 2015, https://www.tms.edu/blog/only-one-life/.

2. Randy Alcorn, *The Law of Rewards* (Carol Stream, IL: Tyndale House Publishers, 2003), 72.

3. "Annie Oakley and the Daring Kaiser Wilhelm II Act," westernhistory.hubpages.com.

4. Tim Chester, *The Ordinary Hero: Living the Cross and the Resurrection* (Nottingham, England: InterVarsity Press, 2009), 192, 207.

5. Woodrow Kroll, *Facing Your Final Job Review: The Judgment Seat of Christ, Salvation, and Eternal Rewards* (Wheaton, IL: Crossway Books, 2008), 44.

6. Alcorn, *The Law of Rewards*, 21.

7. Alcorn, *The Law of Rewards*, 73.

8. Alcorn, *The Law of Rewards*, 106.

9. John Calvin, as cited in Ben Patterson, *Serving God: The Grand Essentials of Work & Worship*, rev. ed. (Downers Grove, IL: InterVarsity Press, 1994), 77.

10. "Arthur Barry: Greatest Jewel Thief," Worlds Ultimate, https://www.worldsultimate.net/arthur-barry.htm.

11. Erwin W. Lutzer, *Your Eternal Reward* (Chicago, IL: Moody Press, 1998), 24.

Chapter 2—Salvation and Rewards

1. Randy Alcorn, *The Law of Rewards* (Carol Stream, IL: Tyndale House Publishers, 2003), 68.

2. Alcorn, *The Law of Rewards*, 68.

3. Alcorn, *The Law of Rewards*, 51.

4. Donald Guthrie, *New Testament Theology* (Downers Grove, IL: InterVarsity Press, 1983), 860-862.

5. Alcorn, *The Law of Rewards*, 96.

Chapter 3—Under Review

1. As cited in "When I Stand at the Judgment Seat," https://bible.org/illustration/when-i-stand-judgment-seat.

2. Erwin W. Lutzer, *Your Eternal Reward* (Chicago, IL: Moody Press, 1998), 115.

3. Lutzer, *Your Eternal Reward*, 115.

4. Woodrow Kroll, *Facing Your Final Job Review: The Judgment Seat of Christ, Salvation, and Eternal Rewards* (Wheaton, IL: Crossway Books, 2008), 95.

5. Paul N. Benware, *Understanding End Times Prophecy* (Chicago, IL: Moody Press, 1995), 182.

6. Posttribulationist George Eldon Ladd says there is no evidence in Scripture that believers will be rewarded before Christ returns. George Eldon Ladd, *The Blessed Hope* (Grand Rapids, MI: Wm. B. Eerdmans Publishing, 1986), 103. Ladd's assertion overlooks Revelation 19, which says the rewarded bride is in heaven with Christ before He returns to Earth.

7. For further information about the timing of the rapture and the future time of tribulation, see Mark Hitchcock, *The End* (Carol Stream, IL: Tyndale House Publishers, 2012).

8. Ladd, *The Blessed Hope*, 103.

9. John F. Walvoord, *The Rapture Question*, rev. ed. (Grand Rapids, MI: Zondervan Publishing House, 1979), 85.

10. Lutzer, *Your Eternal Reward*, 23.

11. Anthony A. Hoekema, *The Bible and the Future* (Grand Rapids, MI: William B. Eerdmans, 1979), 259.

12. Samuel L. Hoyt, "The Judgment Seat of Christ and Unconfessed Sins," *Bibliotheca Sacra* (January-March 1980): 39.

13. Oscar Hammerstein, as cited in Ben Patterson, *Serving God: The Grand Essentials of Work & Worship*, rev. ed. (Downers Grove, IL: InterVarsity Press, 1994), 74.

14. Quoted in Patterson, *Serving God*, 74.

15. Randy Alcorn, *Heaven* (Wheaton, IL: Tyndale House Publishers, 2004), 313.

Chapter 4—Your Dream House

1. Erwin W. Lutzer, *Your Eternal Reward* (Chicago, IL: Moody Press, 1998), 24.

2. The context of this passage looks back to Paul's work in Corinth during his eighteen months there on his second missionary journey (Acts 18:11). Paul had laid the foundation of the church at Corinth, teaching God's Word. He was concerned about what would happen after his departure. He implored those who would lead the church in his absence to build the superstructure of quality spiritual materials that would last. He told them that someday the Lord, at the judgment seat, would evaluate their work of building the church. While this is the interpretation of this passage in its context, I believe there is justification to apply it to the individual lives of believers. John MacArthur says, "The context makes it clear that a broader and more inclusive application is also in mind. The numerous references to 'each man' and 'any man' (vv. 10-18) indicate that the principle applies to every believer. All of us, by what we say and do, to some extent teach the gospel...Every believer is to be a careful builder. We all have the same responsibility" (John MacArthur, *1 Corinthians*, The MacArthur New Testament Commentary [Chicago, IL: Moody Press, 1984], 80-81).

3. John F. Walvoord, *The Church in Prophecy* (Grand Rapids, MI: Zondervan Publishing House, 1964), 149.

4. MacArthur, *1 Corinthians*, 83.

5. Woodrow Kroll, *Facing Your Final Job Review: The Judgment Seat of Christ, Salvation, and Eternal Rewards* (Wheaton, IL: Crossway Books, 2008), 79.

Chapter 5—A Rewarding Q & A

1. Max Lucado, *Max on Life* (Nashville, TN: Thomas Nelson, 2010), 207.

2. D.M. Panton, *The Judgment Seat of Christ* (Hayesville, NC: Schoettle Publishing, 1993), 26.

3. Woodrow Kroll, *Facing Your Final Job Review: The Judgment Seat of Christ, Salvation, and Eternal Rewards* (Wheaton, IL: Crossway Books, 2008), 123-124.

4. H.A. Ironside, *Salvation and Reward: Two Distinct Lines of Truth* (Create Space Independent Publishing Platform, 2015), 45-46.

5. Paul N. Benware, *The Believer's Payday* (Chattanooga, TN: AMG Publishers, 2002), 158-159.

6. Kent Crockett, *Making Today Count for Eternity* (Sisters, OR: Multnomah Publishers, 2001), 85.

7. As cited in "When I Stand at the Judgment Seat," https://bible.org/illustration/when-i-stand-judgment-seat.

8. Max Lucado, *Max on Life* (Nashville, TN: Thomas Nelson, 2010), 207.

9. Randy Alcorn, *The Law of Rewards* (Carol Stream, IL: Moody Press, 1991), 106.

10. Mark Bailey, "Judgment Seat of Christ," in *The Popular Encyclopedia of Bible Prophecy*, gen. eds. Tim LaHaye and Ed Hindson (Eugene, OR: Harvest House Publishers, 2004), 179.

11. Randy Alcorn, *The Law of Rewards* (Carol Stream, IL: Tyndale House Publishers, 2003), 56.

12. Joe Wall, *Going for the Gold: Reward and Loss at the Judgment of Believers* (Chicago, IL: Moody Press, 1991), 119.

13. Samuel L. Hoyt, "The Negative Aspects of the Christian's Judgment," *Bibliotheca Sacra* (April-June 1980): 131.

14. Kroll, *Facing Your Final Job Review*, 105.

15. Erwin W. Lutzer, *Your Eternal Reward* (Chicago, IL: Moody Press, 1998), 34.

16. To make his point that not every believer is an overcomer, Zane Hodges takes the statement in Revelation 2:11 as a figure of speech known as *litotes*, which is "a way of making a positive affirmation by affirming its opposite" (Zane C. Hodges, *Grace in Eclipse* [Corinth, TX: Grace Evangelical Society, 2016], 154). Litotes is basically an obvious understatement. Taking it this way, Hodges translates Revelation 2:11 in this way: "The experience of the overcomer is *radically free* from the second death." But to me, his answer begs the question. Every believer will also be radically free from the second death. Taking Revelation 2:11 as litotes doesn't make his case but reinforces that every believer is an overcomer.

17. Again, Zane Hodges takes Revelation 3:5 as litotes just like Revelation 2:11. He says that what Jesus is saying to the overcomer is "your everlasting name is *supremely secure*." But isn't this true of every believer? Our salvation is everlastingly secure and guaranteed. That's the point.

18. Zane Hodges represents some scholars who hold that the overcomer in Revelation 2–3 is a faithful believer, not every believer (Erwin Lutzer agrees with Hodges—he believes the promise is made to specific individuals within each congregation, not all the believers. See Lutzer, *Your Eternal Reward*, 150). Referring to 1 John 5:4, Hodges says,

> It is true that the Apostle John affirms that "whatever is born of God overcomes the world" and goes on to say that "our faith" is the victory that has overcome the world (1 John 5:4). Moreover, he adds, "Who is he who overcomes the world, but he who believes that Jesus is the Son of God?" (1 John 5:5). Neither statement is in any way synonymous with the statements in Revelation 2 and 3. They are not only found in wholly different books, but also in contexts different from each other. To appeal to the letter of 1 John to interpret the promises of Revelation simply because similar expressions are used is totally invalid. All good interpretation takes place *in context*" (Hodges, *Grace in Eclipse*, 152).

I agree that we must take every passage in its context, and when taken in context the promises to the overcomer in Revelation 2–3 apply to every believer. Also, understanding how the same author uses a given term is part of proper biblical interpretation.

19. John MacArthur, *Revelation 1–11*, The MacArthur New Testament Commentary (Chicago, IL: Moody Press, 1999), 64-65.

20. Lutzer, *Your Eternal Reward*, 27.

Chapter 6—Gaining What You Can't Lose

1. Doug McIntosh, *Life's Greatest Journey* (Chicago, IL: Moody Press, 2000), 196.

2. Randy Alcorn, *Heaven* (Wheaton, IL: Tyndale House Publishers, 2004), 226.

3. Alcorn, *Heaven*, 226-227.

4. Alcorn, *Heaven*, 227.

5. Erwin W. Lutzer, *Your Eternal Reward* (Chicago, IL: Moody Press, 1998), 156.

6. Gordon D. Fee, *The First Epistle to the Corinthians*, The New International Commentary on the New Testament, gen. ed. F.F. Bruce (Grand Rapids, MI: William B. Eerdmans Publishing, 1987), 433.

7. Woodrow Kroll, *Facing Your Final Job Review: The Judgment Seat of Christ, Salvation, and Eternal Rewards* (Wheaton, IL: Crossway Books, 2008), 189.

8. Joe Wall, *Going for the Gold: Reward and Loss at the Judgment of Believers* (Chicago, IL: Moody Press, 1991), 153.

9. Lutzer, *Your Eternal Reward*, 152.

10. Max Lucado, *When Christ Comes* (Nashville, TN: Word Publishing, 1999), 74.

11. Randy Alcorn, *The Law of Rewards* (Carol Stream, IL: Tyndale House Publishers, 2003), xii.

12. J. Dwight Pentecost, *Things to Come* (Grand Rapids, MI: Zondervan Publishing House, 1958), 226.

13. Max Lucado, *Max on Life* (Nashville, TN: Thomas Nelson, 2010), 207.

Chapter 7—Use It or Lose It

1. Letter to General George B. McClellan after the bloody battle of Antietam in 1862. McClellan's lack of activity during the US Civil War irritated Lincoln.

2. Warren W. Wiersbe, *Meeting Yourself in the Parables* (Wheaton, IL: Victor Books, 1979), 14.

3. R. Kent Hughes, *Luke*, vol. 2, Preaching the Word (Wheaton, IL: Crossway Books, 1998), 230.

4. Zane C. Hodges, *Grace in Eclipse: A Study on Eternal Rewards* (Corinth, TX: Grace Evangelical Society, 2016), 132.

5. In Matthew 22:13, after referring to a guest who came to the wedding feast totally unprepared, Jesus said, "Bind him hand and foot, and cast him into the outer darkness; in that place there shall be weeping and gnashing of teeth." Jesus followed those words with another statement: "Many are called, but few are chosen" (Matthew 22:14). Verse 14 indicates that Jesus is referring to a man who has not been chosen—one who is lost and being cast into hell. Zane Hodges, who holds that the man cast into outer darkness is a believer, says,

> Here one must keep firmly in mind that we are dealing with a parable filled with symbolic elements. The man's hands and feet are bound…But no one takes this binding literally, even if it is thought that an unsaved man is in view. Indeed, the wedding garment he lacks is not literal, nor for that matter is the wedding supper itself…The "darkness outside" is a powerful, evocative image for the exclusion he experiences as a result. There is no suggestion here of punishment or torment. The presence of remorse, in the form of weeping and gnashing of teeth, does not in any way require this inference. Indeed, what we actually see in the image itself is a man soundly "trussed up" out on the darkened grounds of the king's private estate, while the banquet hall glows with light and reverberates with the joys of those inside. That is what we actually see. *And that is all…*It is enough to say that the failing Christian has missed a splendid experience of co-reigning with Christ, with all the multiplied joys which that experience implies. It is enough to affirm that he undergoes a significant exclusion from the "light and gladness, joy and honor…which the co-heirs experience with

Christ. Whatever else eternity holds for him, he has at least missed *that*" (Hodges, *Grace in Eclipse*, 126-127).

Hodges goes on to say that the weeping and gnashing of teeth is the remorse of the believer for all that he's lost. He has missed co-heirship with Christ and joined "the crowded ranks of the many who are called to co-heirship and misses the elite number of the few who actually attain it" (Hodges, *Grace in Eclipse*, 128).

It is true that Matthew 22:1-14 and Matthew 24:14-30 are parables, but so is Luke 16, and conservative scholars agree that the rich man is in a literal place called Hades, although various elements are added to the story that are not necessarily literal. The main point, however, is literal. This rich man is in Hades, separated from God and all that is good, and he is in torment. Likewise, "outer darkness" refers to the final destination of unbelievers. The darkness outside is not some place on the grounds of the king's estate, but contrasts with the joy inside the messianic banquet and kingdom from which these men are excluded. Moreover, the words "weeping and gnashing of teeth" are found in Matthew 8:12; 13:42, 50, where they clearly refer to the final condition of unbelievers. Matthew 13:41-42 says, "The Son of Man will send forth His angels, and they will gather out of His kingdom all stumbling blocks, and those who commit lawlessness, and will throw them into the furnace of fire; in that place there will be weeping and gnashing of teeth." Matthew could not be any clearer that the place of "weeping and gnashing of teeth" is a location for people excluded from Christ's kingdom. You can't miss Christ's kingdom and be a Christian. Matthew 13:49-50 says, "So it will be at the end of the age; the angels will come forth and take out the wicked from among the righteous, and will throw them into the furnace of fire; in that place there will be weeping and gnashing of teeth." Matthew says that the "wicked" will be in the place of weeping and gnashing of teeth. This cannot be a reference to a believer. Taking outer darkness and the place of weeping and gnashing of teeth as anything other than hell goes against the usage of these terms by Matthew.

6. John F. Walvoord and Charles H. Dyer, *Matthew*, The John Walvoord Prophecy Commentaries, ed. Philip E. Rawley (Chicago, IL: Moody Publishers, 2013), 343.

7. Charles R. Swindoll, *Insights on Luke*, Swindoll's New Testament Insights (Grand Rapids, MI: Zondervan Publishing House, 2012), 442.

8. John MacArthur, *The Second Coming: Signs of Christ's Return and the End of the Age* (Wheaton, IL: Crossway Books, 1999), 174.

9. Louis A. Barbieri, Jr. "Matthew," *The Bible Knowledge Commentary*, eds. John F. Walvoord and Roy B. Zuck (Wheaton, IL: Victor Books, 1983), 80.

10. John MacArthur, *Luke 18–24*, The MacArthur New Testament Commentary (Chicago, IL: Moody Publishers, 2014), 84

11. Darrell L. Bock, *Luke 9:51–24:53*, Baker Exegetical Commentary on the New Testament, ed. Moises Silva (Grand Rapids, MI: Baker Books, 1996), 1542-1543.

12. Randy Alcorn, *The Law of Rewards* (Carol Stream, IL: Tyndale House Publishers, 2003), 74.

13. MacArthur, *The Second Coming*, 175.

14. Lewis Johnson, as cited in https://s3-us-west-2.amazonaws.com/ sljinstitute production/newtestament/matthew/084_SLJ_Matthew .pdf.

Chapter 8—Your Final Exam

1. Randy Alcorn, *The Law of Rewards* (Carol Stream, IL: Tyndale House Publishers, 2003), 38-39.

2. Tim Chester, *The Ordinary Hero*: *Living the Cross and the Resurrection* (Nottingham, England: InterVarsity Press, 2009), 200.

3. Alcorn, *The Law of Rewards*, 43.

4. Thomas Chalmers, as cited in "No Time to Waste," Know Truth, June 25, 2014, https://www.ktt.org/resources/truth-matters/no -time-waste.

5. R. Kent Hughes, *Hebrews*, vol. 2 (Wheaton, IL: Crossway Books, 1993), 160.

6. Joe Stowell, "The Great Race," http://getmorestrength.org/daily/ the-great-race/.

7. Joe Stowell, "The Great Race."

8. Robert Murray McCheyne, as cited in Derek Thomas, "God-Centered Prayer," Ligonier Ministries, https://www.ligonier.org/ learn/articles/god-centered-prayer/.

9. Erwin W. Lutzer, *Your Eternal Reward* (Chicago, IL: Moody Press, 1998), 92.

10. Donald Coggan, as cited in Elizabeth Manneh, "Hospitality for the Terrified: 5 Simple Ways to Reach Out to Others," Busted Halo, June 26, 2017, https://bustedhalo.com/ministry-resources/hospitality-terrified-5-simple-ways-reach-others.

11. Tony Merida, *Ordinary: How to Turn the World Upside Down* (Nashville, TN: B&H Publishing Group, 2015), 45, 47-48, 55.

12. "Max Lucado Describes the Power of Practicing Hospitality," *Preaching Today*, https://www.preachingtoday.com/illustrations/2011/february/3022111.html.

13. H.A. Ironside, *Illustrations of Bible Truth* (Chicago, IL: Moody, 1945), 33-35.

14. Ben Patterson, *Serving God: The Grand Essentials of Work & Worship*, rev. ed. (Downers Grove, IL: InterVarsity Press, 1994), 167-168.

15. Patterson, *Serving God*, 168.

16. "The Smallness of Our Greatness," Bible.org, https://bible.org/illustration/smallness-our-greatness.

Chapter 9—Your Ultimate Payday

1. Randy Alcorn, *The Law of Rewards* (Carol Stream, IL: Tyndale House Publishers, 2003), 63.

2. Paul N. Benware, *The Believer's Payday* (Chattanooga, TN: AMG Publishers, 2002), 1.

3. Doug McIntosh, *Life's Greatest Journey* (Chicago, IL: Moody Press, 2000), 200-201.

4. John MacArthur holds this view. John MacArthur, *Matthew 16–23*, The MacArthur New Testament Commentary (Chicago, IL: Moody Press, 1988), 214.

5. Erwin W. Lutzer, *Your Eternal Reward* (Chicago, IL: Moody Press, 1998), 15, 24.

6. Nicholas Kristof, "What Monkeys Can Teach Us About Fairness," *The New York Times*, June 3, 2017, https://www.nytimes.com/2017/06/03/opinion/sunday/what-monkeys-can-teach-us-about-fairness.html.

7. "Not Now But Later," Know Truth, July 7, 2015, https://www.ktt .org/resources/truth-matters/not-now-later.

8. "John Wesley and George Whitefield," *The Christian Excavator,* October 21, 2012, https://christianexcavator.com/2012/10/21/ john-wesley-and-george-whitefield/.

9. Leslie B. Flynn, *Keep On Keeping On* (Carlsbad, CA: Magnus Press, 2005), 104.

10. Flynn, *Keep On Keeping On,* 106.

Chapter 10—The Grand Bargain

1. William Grimslaw, as cited in Robert J. Morgan, *On This Day in Christian History: 365 Amazing and Inspiring Stories About Saints, Martyrs, and Heroes* (Nashville, TN: Thomas Nelson, 1997), May 17.

2. Some claim the story about the Shackleton ad is a myth. Colin Schultz, "Shackleton Probably Never Took Out an Ad Seeking Men for a Hazardous Journey," *Smithsonian.com,* September 10, 2013, https://www.smithsonianmag.com/smart-news/shackleton -probably-never-took-out-an-ad-seeking-men-for-a-hazardous -journey-5552379. While I have not been able to positively confirm the historicity of the ad, all would agree that the story of the ad does accurately express the danger the expedition posed.

3. Ben Patterson, *Muscular Faith* (Carol Stream, IL: Salt River, 2011), 77-79.

4. Patterson, *Muscular Faith,* 79-80.

5. Patterson, *Muscular Faith,* 80.

6. Tony Evans, *Tony Evans' Book of Illustrations* (Chicago, IL: Moody Publishers, 2009), 256-257.

Appendix One—Answers to a Few More Questions

1. Warren Wiersbe, *The Bible Exposition Commentary: New Testament,* vol. 2 (Wheaton, IL: Victor Books, 1989), 621.

2. Erwin W. Lutzer, *Your Eternal Reward* (Chicago, IL: Moody Press, 1998), 167.

3. Lutzer, *Your Eternal Reward,* 166-167.

STEPS TO PEACE WITH GOD

1. RECOGNIZE GOD'S PLAN—PEACE AND LIFE

The message in this book stresses that God loves you and wants you to experience His peace and life.

The BIBLE says, "For God so loved the world that He gave His only begotten Son, that whoever believes in Him should not perish but have everlasting life." *John 3:16, NKJV*

2. REALIZE OUR PROBLEM—SEPARATION FROM GOD

People choose to disobey God and go their own way. This results in separation from God.

The BIBLE says, "For all have sinned and fall short of the glory of God." *Romans 3:23, NKJV*

3. RESPOND TO GOD'S REMEDY—THE CROSS OF CHRIST

God sent His Son to bridge the gap. Christ did this by paying the penalty of our sins when He died on the cross and rose from the grave.

The BIBLE says, "But God shows his love for us in that while we were still sinners, Christ died for us." *Romans 5:8, ESV*

4. RECEIVE GOD'S SON—LORD AND SAVIOR

You cross the bridge into God's family when you ask Christ to come into your life.

The BIBLE says, "But to all who did receive him, who believed in his name, he gave the right to become children of God." *John 1:12, ESV*

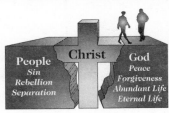

THE INVITATION IS TO:

REPENT (turn from your sins), ASK for God's forgiveness, and by faith RECEIVE Jesus Christ into your heart and life and follow Him in obedience as your Lord and Savior.

PRAYER OF COMMITMENT

"Dear God, I know that I am a sinner. I want to turn from my sins, and I ask for Your forgiveness. I believe that Jesus Christ is Your Son. I believe He died for my sins and that You raised Him to life. I want Him to come into my heart and to take control of my life. I want to trust Jesus as my Savior and follow Him as my Lord from this day forward. In Jesus' Name, amen."

If you are committing your life to Christ, please let us know!

Billy Graham Evangelistic Association
1 Billy Graham Parkway, Charlotte, NC 28201-0001
1-877-2GRAHAM (1-877-247-2426)
BillyGraham.org/commitment